SPIRIT WARS

*The Power of His Might
Against The Rulers of
The Darkness of This World*

SPIRIT WARS

David M. Griffis

CLEVELAND, TENNESSEE 37311

Scripture quotations marked *NKJV* are from *The New King James Version*. Copyright © 1979, 1980, 1982, Thomas Nelson Inc., Publishers. Used by permission.

Scripture quotations marked *NEB* are from *The New English Bible*. © The Delegates of Oxford University Press and The Syndics of the Cambridge University Press 1961, 1970. Reprinted by permission.

Library of Congress Catalog Card Number: 94-065247

ISBN: 0871488213

Copyright © 1994 by Pathway Press
Cleveland, Tennessee 37311
All Rights Reserved

Printed in the United States of America

Dedicated

To those who have given me heritage and value:
My maternal grandfather, country preacher, farmer, philosopher
My parents, a clergyman and wife in whom there is no guile
My wife, who brings strength where I have weakness
My son and daughter, in whom I delight and marvel

Contents

Foreword 9

Preface 11

Acknowledgments 13

Introduction 15

1. New Age: An Old Enemy 25

2. Secular Humanism: The Death of Humanity 37

3. The Occult: Wickedness in High Places 47

4. Science Falsely So Called 61

5. Demons: Satan's Evil Henchmen 67

6. Angels: God's Messenger Warriors 75

7. The Weapons of Our Warfare 87

8. Utterance Through Preaching: God's Chosen Weapon 97

9. Pulling Down Strongholds and Bringing Into Captivity 107

10. Standing: The Power of Waiting 117

11. The Captain of Our Salvation 123

12. The Final Battle: The Triumph of the Lamb 131

Bibliography 139

Foreword

Nearly 2,000 years ago, the apostle Paul warned that the church would face perilous times in the last days. Today the church is experiencing those perilous times as it is confronted by the onslaughts of the New Age movement, secular humanism, the occult, evolutionary science, and the sensual tendencies of the mass media. As author David M. Griffis points out, there is more than flesh and blood behind the events we are witnessing today. The church is locked in battle with sinister powers of darkness. We are engaged in a spirit war with enemies of the Cross—the leader of which is Satan himself.

This book systematically expounds the teachings and practices of these foes of the church and reveals the deception that underlies them. They are exposed, not as opponents of flesh and blood, but as spiritual principalities and powers that cannot be engaged with carnal weapons. If we are to be triumphant against the enemies of Christianity, we must understand that spiritual battles can be fought only with spiritual weapons. The author details the mighty weapons in the Christian arsenal and shows the reader how to use them not only defensively but also offensively to pull down strongholds of Satan. He shows how to go on the spiritual offensive and when to wait on the Lord.

This work is more than just another sensational treatment designed to sell books. David Griffis has carefully researched the subject to give the church a biblically based, sensible, and effective approach to spiritual warfare. The underlying theme of this book is the biblical truth of the church's ultimate triumph over Satan's empire of evil as we follow Christ, the Captain of our salvation. *Spirit Wars* gives the reader God's plan for the triumphant, victorious life to be lived by real Christians.

David M. Griffis is well qualified to write this book for the church. He is a son of the church who has joined in many spiritual battles against the foes of God's people. He has served the church ably as an evangelist, pastor, and state director of youth and Christian education in the states of Oklahoma, Georgia, and South Carolina. A graduate of Lee College, David presently serves as the assistant director of Youth and Christian Education for the Church of God, Cleveland, Tennessee.

I commend this important book to the reader. My prayer is that it will encourage Christians everywhere to join in the last-day battle with renewed insight into Satan's devices and the strong assurance that God's church will triumph over all the forces of evil confronting us.

Dr. Robert White
First Assistant General Overseer
Church of God

Preface

Satan has a diverse arsenal from which to launch his attacks against Christ's church. In this volume, the New Age movement, secular humanism, the occult with its bizarre trappings, false science, the sensual motivation of modern media, and other enemies of the Cross are exposed—not as opponents of flesh and blood but as the spiritual principalities and powers they are.

God's plan for the triumphant, victorious life to be lived by real Christians is revealed as the author deals with spiritual weaponry. He shows us how to go on the spiritual offensive, when to wait on the Lord, the fact that Christ is Captain of our salvation, and the biblical truth of ultimate Christian triumph over Satan's empire of evil.

Take hope as you are assured once again that the spiritual battles and obstacles confronting true Christianity in these latter days fade into insignificance before the power of Jesus Christ our Lord.

T. David Sustar, Director
Youth and Christian Education Department

Acknowledgements

I want to thank the many people who helped make this book a reality. T. David Sustar, my friend and colleague, encouraged me a number of years ago to pursue this area of interest and offered constant encouragement. Larry A. Bergeron, friend and Christian literature expert, gave much-needed counsel and advice. Tom George, who edited the book, is one of the very best in his profession and was of great help. Lonzo T. Kirkland, a fine professional, did a masterful job with the cover design. Donald Pemberton and Ron Wood listened and offered sound advice. A special thanks to Dr. Robert O'Bannon, a superb scientist, friend, and student of God's Word, who examined and edited the chapter on evolution. My pastor, David Bishop, the best of shepherds, who exemplifies a real spiritual warrior, was an inspiration. Judy, my wife and best friend, was always there and, like a good wife should be, was a "sounding board" who responded with frankness and honesty. Wanda Martin, my secretary, with godly patience and clerical expertise, typed and retyped the manuscript and helped the entire project go smoothly. To all these dear friends, I say, "Thank you!"

Introduction

Something evil is afoot on this earth, and it has been for thousands of years. Amid the glitter, tinsel, and bright lights of Satan's earthly palaces of pleasure lie the shattered lives and hopeless faces of a human race in bitter bondage to sin. A long look at the earth reveals a panorama of people in abject poverty; riddled with disease; victims of war, famine, and upheavals of nature; and searching desperately for a balm to heal their wounded souls.

The latter half of the 20th century has produced a myriad of religious movements promising solace and hope for the hurting peoples of the earth. Many of these movements mesmerize their followers by changing their lives with bizarre behavior and religious belief totally contrary to the Word of God as found in Scripture. Movements such as New Age, humanism, the occult, and evolutionary science have found in today's technological, media-oriented society a fertile garden to plant their vile seeds and reap their dark harvest. The movie moguls, advertising tycoons, and merchandising magnates have found these evil movements to be a rich source of easy wealth. The movements themselves, while gaining their footholds, have cloaked themselves in a message of harmlessness; and they appeal to the youth of our time to permanently ensure their longevity. Their grip has become large and powerful. To the casual observer, it seems they are here to stay. The time has come for the truth to be told. The corruption that surrounds us is not the work of flesh and blood despite their sophistication and technology. The unbridled greed and unchecked violence that fills the earth is more than the actions of men with no morals. The river of filth flooding the earth has a source that has effectively done what the apostle Paul said Satan could do: "Satan himself is transformed into an angel of light" (2 Corinthians 11:14).

Paul's admonition to the Ephesians has powerful relevance for us today: "For our fight is not against human foes, but against cosmic powers, against the authorities and potentates of this dark world, against the superhuman forces of evil in the heavens" (Ephesians 6:12, *NEB*).

We tend to mistake who our enemy really is. We have trouble identifying the source of our spiritual battles. Because we are housed in robes of flesh, we react to our senses. What we hear and see comes from a physical source, so it is only natural for us to label it as the problem. Our real enemy, Satan, is no fool. He knows he is dealing with human beings much better than we know we are dealing with spirits. Consequently, he roams freely. The Bible bears this out very plainly: "Be sober, be vigilant; because your adversary the devil, as a roaring lion, walketh about, seeking whom he may devour" (1 Peter 5:8).

Anyone who has studied the nature of lions knows they look first for the weak, crippled, young, or unsuspecting for their prey. Once they find their victim, they begin their subtle and careful approach. Just before the charge they tense and then attack with all their ferocity. So Satan seeks his victims. To catch and devour those already ensnared by sin and weakened by the effects of their iniquity is no great task. But he also looks for prayerless, carnal Christians who have neglected the Word of God and the admonition to "add to your faith virtue; and to virtue knowledge; and to knowledge temperance; and to temperance patience; and to patience godliness; and to godliness brotherly kindness; and to brotherly kindness charity" (2 Peter 1:5-7). In other words, he looks for Christians who failed to grow and mature through a discipleship process that takes effort and time. He also looks for the discouraged and downtrodden. He seeks out those whose lives have become disrupted by tragedy, loss, or events beyond their control. Therefore, he is never at a loss for people to victimize.

He also attacks the strong and healthy. Lions in Africa have been seen attacking full-grown Cape buffalo bulls, one of the most powerful beasts of the African plains. Though the Cape buffalo can run and fight and has incredible power, the lions band together and catch the unsuspecting buffalo downwind, sever his hamstring muscles, get him on the ground, and then crush his windpipe and jugular vein with powerful jaws. A gruesome picture, yet so is the devil's attack on the strong. In these last days this is a truth of special consequence. Because of the power of the media and the smallness of our world through increase of knowledge, the devil and his allies in the spirit world are attacking many strong and productive servants of God. His strategy is to destroy soldiers of the Cross who have had a great impact on the world and have influenced many for Christ so that their falling will bring discouragement and disillusionment to other Christians. Also, he is trying to weaken the effect of the gospel message on an already cynical and disbelieving world.

Have you noticed how fast bad news travels, especially if it is the news of an evangelist or clergyman who goes astray? And the world seems to laugh and almost enjoy the fall of those who are engaged in ministry. Like cackling hyenas standing around the kill of a pride of lions, waiting to devour the remains after the lions have gorged themselves, so the world laughs at the downfall of Christians. When noted evangelists have succumbed to moral failures and illicit business practices in recent years, the late-night comedians used these sad tragedies in their comic routines for months and their fans roared with delight. What is happening here? Surely something very sinister and evil is taking place.

Hollywood and the film and television industry attack Christianity constantly and laugh at moral standards. A few years ago a television actress portrayed a woman who chose to have an illegitimate child and presented this as a viable, decent option with no moral implications at all. When the vice president of the United States condemned this portrayal while making a speech on family and moral values, he was berated more than any public figure in recent memory. The media tried to portray the second-highest elected official of the United States of America as a fool because he stood for decency and biblical values. And this is not the only case. In most Hollywood productions, clergy and Christians are portrayed as fanatics, mentally unstable, and often as homicidal psychopaths. The devil is working constantly to undermine and thwart the efforts of world evangelization. He attempts to make the message of the Cross "of none effect."

Satan is constantly attacking the family. The family was God's first institution (Genesis 2:24). It is one of the things the devil hates the most. His attacks on the family are taking an increasingly subtle turn. It is easy to see what neglect, hatred, infidelity, lies, and selfishness can do to a family; but we need to understand we are not dealing with flesh and blood. There are underlying causes we must understand, and they require spiritual insight. Spiritual warfare requires spiritual knowledge and looking beyond the things that are seen.

The power of media on our family structures cannot be underestimated. Wholesome programming, good films and books, and educational enlightenment can be beneficial for the family. However, most of media does not present this type of material.

Some estimates say the average American television stays on seven and one-half hours per day. This is almost one-third of the day. Even when it is not being watched, the background sounds provide for assimilation of undesirable knowledge. Children reaching their teen years have seen thousands of murders, assaults, adulterous relationships, thefts, drug usage, and a host of other unsavory things. Some may retort, "Let them see it all; they shouldn't be sheltered from the real world." But has this "real world" been created and nurtured by the media blitz of evil? Many people believe it has. Even secular experts are realizing television and the film industry have been left unbridled too long and that the rampage of violence sweeping our nation and the world has a protagonist behind it. They say there is no way the immature young minds of the nation's children can properly deal with the violence and lust portrayed on the screen. A knowledge of God's Word tells us Christians that no one, at any age, can feed on a diet of garbage and not be affected. Our enemy "the roaring lion" is well aware of these factors, and he promotes evil and cynicism toward Christianity.

18

Satan's attack on the Christian world also reaches into the area of overindulgence and greed for personal gain. Western culture has become very greedy. A desire to "get gain" seems a part of the psyche of modern man. In fact, most Western economies are based on supply and demand with an emphasis on new and better. Many products become obsolete after a brief life span. The accumulation of wealth and possessions is a time-consuming activity. The paradox is almost comical yet incredibly sad. We have more time- and labor-saving devices than ever before, and yet we have less time to be real. Everybody in the family complains, "Nobody has time to listen to me!" Our microwave ovens, automatic dishwashers, remote control music and televisions, refrigerators with automatic ice and water dispensers, and all our push-button world have left us with more exhaustion and less time for each other. Something isn't right. We have forgotten our mission as Christians on this earth.

When the lion attacks, he often rakes his sharp claws across the eyes of his prey and blinds it. The prey, consequently, is doomed. The Bible says in 2 Corinthians 4:4 that "the god of this world hath blinded the minds of them which believe not." Satan seeks to blind us to real riches and what really matters. It is again time to consider the business of eternity; we need a revival of eternal consideration. Christ had much to say about the dangers of materialism; it was one of His most-often-preached topics. It is one of man's greatest areas of weakness. On the battlefield of spiritual warfare, it is a vulnerable area—a bare spot in the armor.

Christ said the deceitfulness of riches would choke the seed of the Word in a man's heart and the seed would not mature and bear fruit (Matthew 13:22). In Luke 18:24 He said, "How hardly shall they that have riches enter into the kingdom of God!" It is important to understand Christ was talking about the love of riches and the consuming passion for their gain. The Bible is full of wealthy men and women who benefited the kingdom of God. Joseph of Arimathea, Lydia, Zacchaeus, Abraham, and Job, to name a few, were people who willingly used their riches to glorify God. Here is the key: they loved God more than their riches. Upon his conversion Zacchaeus gave half his goods to feed the poor and restored fourfold any wealth he had received through unethical business practices (Luke 19:8).

The great danger in the spiritual war of the last days lies in the infatuation with getting gain to the neglect of everything that is more important. The simplicity of life and the beauty of love can be smothered and lost, replaced by something that will not last—made of plastic, metal, or wood. Though this love of things has always plagued mankind, its powerful proliferation in these end times tells us it is part of Satan's last-day prowl, and he doesn't mind walking through the department stores, car lots, and subdivisions.

Finally, there is an attack on our time! Prayer—real prayer—takes time. Reading the Bible and studying the meaning of Scripture takes time. Listening to the cares and concerns of our children and our spouses demands quality time. Meditating and bringing our thoughts into captivity to the obedience of Christ takes concentrated, undisturbed time. These uses of time are richly rewarding for the family, the body of Christ, and the individual. When the family unit is strengthened, each member of the family is strengthened. When the family is functioning as a strong unit, the church, which is made up of families, becomes vital, healthy, and productive. The church then can fulfill its biblical responsibilities of evangelization, discipleship, and nurture. And the individual, as a unique member of the body of Christ, can benefit and grow in Christian maturity. With these marvelous possibilities, it is understandable why one of Satan's greatest tactics of spiritual warfare is to steal time. He is a master thief, with a horrible intent. Jesus said, "The thief cometh not, but for to steal, and to kill, and to destroy: I am come that they might have life, and that they might have it more abundantly" (John 10:10).

We must guard our time with all diligence and use it as a precious commodity. Some things can wait, but the precious lives of children, the affections of a loving spouse, the nurture of God's Word, the strength of prayer, and the family cannot wait—and they take time.

We are engaged in a great war with a powerful enemy. It is a war of the spirit and not of the flesh, though its consequences direly affect the flesh. It is a war that will affect the panorama of eternity, and it must be viewed as such.

Though the war in the spirit realm has been raging since Satan's fall, this war has intensified manyfold as we approach the end of earthly human history. As God's prophetic plans concerning the church, the nation of Israel, and the world come to a climactic end, the powers of darkness are exercising their full strength and are on the attack. Every theme and strategy that can be devised against what is good, holy, righteous, pure, and Christlike is being unleashed.

Many churches have fallen prey to secularization. Numerical and financial growth has become their goal, rather than numerical growth coupled with total discipleship development and evangelical fervor as found in the Book of Acts. To some, the teaching and preaching of sound doctrine—such as the efficacy of the blood of Christ; sanctification through the blood of Christ, the Word, and the Holy Spirit; the baptism in the Holy Spirit to provide power for service; the second coming of Christ; the power of intercessory prayer; and a Word-oriented church—have become taboo and labeled outdated. The "expert" analysts tell us the church must become a potpourri of possibilities and offer a supermarket gospel. In other words, the church is to be shopped like a mall, with potential parishioners taking what they like and if nothing suits their fancy going elsewhere to tantalize their taste buds. Sadly, the analysts' picture is probably a true portrait for much of the world. But the Word of God does not allow the alteration of truth or the molding of messages to please the ears of the masses. What has really happened here?

Perhaps the best explanation can be found in 2 Timothy 4:3, 4: "For the time will come when they will not endure sound doctrine; but after their own lusts shall they heap to themselves teachers, having itching ears; and they shall turn away their ears from the truth, and shall be turned unto fables."

Again, the war is one in the spirit realm. Demonic forces are swaying the masses. Because we are media-oriented, we now have a generation that wants entertainment. To feel good for the moment seems the goal of our times. Israel once adopted this philosophy in the days of Isaiah. Their cry became "Let us eat and drink; for to morrow we shall die" (Isaiah 22:13). God's answer to them was "Surely this iniquity shall not be purged from you till ye die" (v. 14). They had become so self-centered and humanistic in their thinking that only death would end their fatalistic approach to life.

Is there hope for the children of Adam's race in these last days? Yes! God is not only the God of hope and precious promises, He is also the God of fulfilled hope and true promises. "We are more than conquerors through him that loved us" (Romans 8:37).

In order for us to fight victoriously in these spirit wars, we must understand our Enemy. Paul warns us not to be "ignorant of his devices" (2 Corinthians 2:11). It is important to understand him—his past, present, and future. We should have a knowledge of his purposes, techniques, and power, as well as his limitations, weaknesses, and fears. We should know something of the demon realm and the highly structured system of demonic organization and its chain of command as found in the Scripture. Fantasizing and sensationalism concerning demons and their powers are useless in real spiritual warfare. We must separate fact from fiction and be scriptural in our approach.

Poor is the soldier and vulnerable is the commander who doesn't know and understand his enemy. On the battlefield he will be taken advantage of by the enemy.

God has given the believer weapons, advantages, and strengths through Christ that are far beyond the capabilities of the Enemy, for "greater is he that is in you, than he that is in the world" (1 John 4:4). Warriors of the Cross, therefore, must be willing to train and discipline themselves to be successful in the spiritual arena.

Because of our strengths in Christ, Satan's tactics are those of subtlety. Words like *subtle, cunning, deceptive, hidden,* and *crafty* describe him perfectly.

Let us expose him as the enemy he is. There are many chinks in his armor, and our weapons are mighty through God (2 Corinthians 10:4). Do not be misled; we can, through God, defeat the foes of darkness. We have been identified as "the light of the world" (Matthew 5:14). Christ best describes the power of light: "And this is the condemnation, that light is come into the world, and men loved darkness rather than light, because their deeds were evil. For every one that doeth evil hateth the light, neither cometh to the light, lest his deeds should be reproved. But he that doeth truth cometh to the light, that his deeds may be made manifest, that they are wrought in God" (John 3:19-21).

23

CHAPTER 1

NEW AGE: AN OLD ENEMY

Of all the religious and spiritual movements of modern times, perhaps none has captivated this media-oriented generation like the New Age movement. Because its bizarre nature lends itself to the world of fantasy and sensationalism, it has become one of Hollywood's favorite subjects. This, coupled with the fact that many stars of stage and screen have personally embraced it as their life's philosophy and religious experience, has given the New Age movement unparalleled exposure and growth today.

What is the average person's response to the New Age movement? There is a dichotomy of reaction to this movement of mystery. Many of the unchurched younger generation who have no training in Evangelical principles are fascinated by the mystical nature of this religion. Other young people, even those with conservative Christian backgrounds, are entranced by their curiosity and view the New Age as both harmless and somewhat entertaining. Some people who are constantly searching for fulfillment have embraced the New Age readily.

Many dedicated Christians have a paranoia concerning the New Age movement. Insecure in their beliefs, and not knowing the intent, direction, and modus operandi involved, they are on a constant "witch-hunt" for evidence of New Age infiltration.

God is a God of light, not of darkness. He doesn't want His people to be ignorant concerning that which is harmful. Let us examine the beginning, history, and current direction of the New Age movement. A careful look will reveal something sinister is at work. Powers of darkness are guiding a movement that is not "new" at all but has been in the business of deception and destruction for centuries.

To understand New Age philosophy, we must understand it is a religion of combined ingredients. Hinduism, Buddhism, Zen, Gnosticism, Spiritualism, transcendentalism, and the ancient paganism of the Greeks and Romans all played important roles in the formation of the New Age movement. Briefly, let us place each of these elements in their definitive historical role.

Hinduism, which predates Buddhism by at least 1,000 years, stresses reincarnation, ancestor worship, and the gathering of karma. The Hindu religion embraces monotheism (the worship of one God), polytheism (the worship of many gods), and pantheism (everything or "all is god").

Buddhism began in India approximately 2,500 years ago when a monk named Siddhartha Gautama taught many followers who began to call him the Buddha, or "the enlightened one." Today Buddhism boasts 500 million adherents around the world, most of whom live

NEW AGE: AN OLD ENEMY

in Asia, though many have immigrated to the West. Buddhism has been labeled as "practical atheism." Buddhists teach that rather than there being a personal God, God is more a process of becoming. They teach that salvation is found through a self-effort process called the "Eightfold Path." The process includes right belief, right feelings, right speech, right conduct, right livelihood, right effort, right memory, and right meditation. Buddhists believe in reincarnation and teach that when the process is complete, ignorance is eliminated, the cycle of rebirth is over, and the person enters "nirvana," a state of perpetual bliss.

Zen, which is a Japanese word meaning meditation, is a primary element of New Age thinking. A part of the Chinese religion of Taoism, Zen embraces the two principles of *yin* and *yang*. The force of yin is peaceful acceptance, and the force of yang is the principle of activity. This religion of meditation teaches that all is in the mind.

Gnosticism was a problem in New Testament times. This evil philosophy permeates much of modern thinking and is a building block of the New Age movement. Gnosticism comes from the Greek word *gnosis*, meaning "in the know." Simply put, Gnostics teach that the spirit is good and the flesh is evil. They teach that the first God came from the good spirit world and produced many finite beings. They teach that the Creator God of the Bible came from these beings and created the natural or evil world. Gnostics believe the spirit remains pure even if the flesh does evil. One can easily see this belief could lead to unrestrained indulgence and moral decay.

Transcendentalism, with its philosophy of meditation for enlightenment, believes truth is derived through intuition and thus all dogmatism and authority-based religion is to be rejected.

27

SPIRIT WARS

Spiritualism, with its practice of contacting the dead through mediums and seances, has played an integral role in the New Age movement. Practitioners reportedly summon the spirits of long-dead personages who supposedly give them guidance and direction in their lives.

Paganism, from both the ancient Greek Hellenists and Romans, has played a role in the multifaceted New Age movement. Rituals, myths, gods, goddesses, and mythical beasts all are accepted as a part of ancient and modern truth.

These elements teach us that the New Age is not new at all, but old and satanic, for it does not glorify the God of the Bible, nor does it accept His Son, Jesus, as the only way of salvation. On the contrary, the God of Scripture is considered by the New Age movement to be just another cosmic player on the stage of the universe. Some consider Him a minor player, and the Gnostics teach that Jesus never became flesh but only appeared as such.

Three areas of particular focus that should concern Christians as far as New Age growth is concerned are the mass media, educational material, and the pollution of Christian doctrine with elements of New Age philosophy.

Movies and television programming thrive on material featuring futuristic space beings who come into contact with many different forms of cosmic powers and force fields. "The Force" in the *Star Wars* trilogy had a good side and a dark side. In a popular Hollywood movie, a farmer hears voices instructing him to build a baseball diamond in his cornfield so long-dead baseball heroes can return and play.

A popular theme of recent years has been the "ghosts" of the dead who purportedly exist and are active in the everyday lives of people they knew before death. Some are sent back by heavenly deities to perform tasks as penance to allow them permanent entry into heaven. One "ghost" in a popular Hollywood film stayed on the earth after his death to protect his live-in girlfriend from the evils of a deceitful criminal friend. Because this "ghost" had a good nature—although he had lived in a relationship of fornication and cursed frequently—beams of light took him into paradise when his mission was completed.

The message of New Age media is not a message of redemption from sin through the vicarious death of Christ on the cross, but rather it is a message of goodwill, good intentions, and humanism that allows anyone entry into a glorious eternal presence. It is damnable heresy at its worst. It completely leaves out scriptural truth. Christ said, "He that entereth not by the door into the sheepfold, but climbeth up some other way, the same is a thief and a robber" (John 10:1). The New Testament is plain in its requirements for salvation and eternal life. In Acts 4:12 we read, "Neither is there salvation in any other: for there is none other name under heaven given among men, whereby we must be saved."

In spite of the truth of the Bible, the giants of the entertainment industry still put forth their cloaked lies about eternal destiny. Children and young people are especially vulnerable to these types of film, for their young and fertile minds are drawn to excitement and fantasy, and the grip of this danger is very real in their lives.

These are but a few examples of film entertainment that, through fantasy, puts forth the New Age notions that there are many deities, that there are good and bad forces, not a personal God men are accountable to or a real devil determined to ensnare the souls of men. The theory of spiritism and the contacting of the dead, strictly forbidden in Scripture (Deuteronomy 18:10-12), are presented as good and natural and as part of the unseen world. The ideas of eternal punishment and eternal reward are not only overlooked, but in these types of popular films they don't even exist.

The cartoons watched by our children, which once contained comical characters involved in slapstick humor, have turned to a darker subject matter. Fantasy beings, with unbelievable power, now fill the Saturday morning screens. Though good may triumph over evil in these cartoons, notice that good uses the mediums of magic and enchantment to gain victory.

Some people in Evangelical and Pentecostal circles blind themselves to this reality. They think their children and youth are not affected by New Age media. They view it as harmless entertainment, like fairy tales or the make-believe stories of their childhood. It is time we understand our Enemy is neither harmless nor make-believe. Perhaps the reason people don't feel committed to church and religious activities like they once did is that their minds have become fogged with false truth and they have been hypnotized into a false sense of well-being and no longer fear God.

We have raised a generation whose knowledge of truth is clouded by televised fantasy and unbridled violence. They now raise their children on the same diet of media poison. No wonder we are fulfilling the prophecy of Christ, who said, "But as the days of Noah were, so also will the coming of the Son of Man be" (Matthew 24:37, *NKJV*). In the days of Noah the earth was "corrupt" and "filled with violence" (Genesis 6:11), and "God saw that the wickedness of man was great in the earth, and that every imagination of the thoughts of his heart was only evil continually" (v. 5).

NEW AGE: AN OLD ENEMY

Books, from comic books to best-selling novels, are filled with New Age ideology. Sections of popular bookstores are dedicated to science fiction, New Age material, and bizarre comics. Trading cards of these fantasy characters make up an industry that makes millions.

Imagine that! The New Age movement, which promises to make the earth a paradise, has become the money-maker of the last quarter of the 20th century. While true Christianity would change the desire of men's hearts in order for them to help those in need, New Age promotions waste millions of dollars on pure fantasy, dollars that could have filled the hunger-bloated bellies of the starving masses of the world.

Another terrible truth of the New Age fantasy media is that it cloaks the truth about the real consequences its practitioners must face. Error in doctrine is never right just because it is taught in sincerity and is believed by those who teach it. A child's mind fed this kind of diet can become callous to the truth of the gospel. The early years of life are the formative years when truth must be digested. The New Age apostles have targeted the tender ones of our society by using things that quickly fascinate the young. Children love cartoons, so what appeared for years to be innocent cartoon media became the forum for New Age indoctrination.

Young people, especially teens, love adventure and music. Adventure movies are filled with New Age philosophy, and bookstores sell billions of dollars' worth of comic books and science fiction novels to teenagers.

Secular music is a medium that has found a vehicle in the New Age philosophy. There is even a New Age division of music now identified along with gospel, country, pop, and rock. Music is a tool the devil likes best, and in the propagation of the New Age philosophy he has used it to its fullest. Before Satan's fall, according to Ezekiel, the devil was a very musical being. Ezekiel 28:13, 14 tells us when he was created as an "anointed cherub" there was within him "tabrets" and "pipes." The devil has often taken the beauty of music and twisted it for his intents. Whether it was the music of the seductive dance of Salome that so filled Herod with lust that the death of John the Baptist by decapitation resulted, or whether it is the modern-day "death metal" music by drug-crazed rock musicians that has been blamed for teen suicides, the devil can and does use music. It has become common for Christians who speak out against the devil's music to be labeled fanatic and old-fashioned, but that doesn't alter the fact that here is eminent danger.

Typically, New Age music elevates nature, animals, and elements and calls for harmony in the universe. Of course, the real Creator of the universe and all of nature is left out entirely. This is a music of meditation, and the human character is just an element to be at one with the world. Peace seems to be the objective, but there can be no real peace without God and righteousness.

The surge of New Age thought filling the mass media is clearing the stage for the rise of the anti-Christian force in the world. There must be an awakening of sincere Christians to this eminent danger.

The problem is that, as a rule, people trust what they see and hear. They trust it because it is perceived through their senses. The times are no longer simple. Once, faith was passed down from parents to children, and belief was based on God's Word, which was the premise of governmental law, business operations, school and education, and almost everything else in our culture. Not so now—a real culture change is taking place. Determining right from wrong, according to current laws and an impotent judicial system, has become very cloudy. Business is built on profit margins and not service to society. Education, with its foundation of humanism and the teaching of evolution, has failed in the teaching of biblical Christian values. A philosophy like the New Age finds acceptability in all segments of the foundational institutions of our society, and with the backing of the media it has had unprecedented growth.

A great tragedy of our time is that there has been an infiltration of New Age thought in modern education. Curriculum produced with no Judeo-Christian values lends itself easily to this kind of manipulation.

I have interviewed public-school teachers in the United States from five different states in the South, the Midwest, and the North who tell of the state-sponsored seminars that teach the value of transcendental meditation and how to use this technique to quiet and calm children. One teacher described being taught by a meditational teacher in a state-sponsored seminar on how to contact a spirit helper as a resource of strength.

One of the most alarming things being pushed by the federal government is the "Idea Seminars." These seminars, which have been protested by several Christian organizations, are set up in various states for public-school teachers, and in them they are trained on how to deal with so-called right-wing Christian extremists—in other words, how to thwart the work of the church and its members who believe in things like the right to pray publicly, the biblical account of Creation, sexual abstinence before marriage, the evil of abortion, decency in literature, and the sacredness of family. In reality, the label they have placed on us compliments us. First, we are "right," because the Bible we believe and the God we serve is right. Second, we have been lifted up on "wings" of love above our sinful state through the power of redemption by Him who has healing in His wings (Malachi 4:2). Third, we are Christians and we have no apologies to offer. We love Christ, we serve Christ, we want to emulate Christ; thus we are Christians. And, yes, we are "extremists," for we are extremely fortunate, extremely saved, extremely happy, and extremely determined to stand for what is right.

A great danger the New Age ideology fosters is the acceptance of a neutral stand on God himself and who He is. New Age thinking allows for a multiplicity of deities. Though it is very frightening, there is growing in our society a neutrality about the idea of God. People are saying, "God is whatever you wish Him to be." Many well-intentioned people now believe all religions are correct, that God is simply identified by different cultures and societies in different ways. Freedom of religion, which is a noble concept of democracy, has led to freedom from the truth. In the free nations of the world, especially in the West, there has been a deluge of immigration from Asian and other cultures where Buddhism, Hinduism, Spiritualism, and other New Age and occult religions are prominent. Because many so-called Christians had little or no training and Christian discipline in their lives, they not only didn't know what to believe, but they also were easily led as converts to the mysticism of Eastern religion. Therefore, the New Age movement, with its worship of almost everything and its takeover of the powerful institutions of America, has gained millions of converts.

We are in a spiritual war against the elements of falsehood and deception. Satan is behind this battle. He desires for the bastions of fundamental Christian teaching and evangelization to be destroyed. During this century most of world evangelization for Christ has been done by the Western Hemisphere. As the Victorian Age ended in England, and as Europe, through two world wars, drifted into religious apostasy, the task of evangelization fell to the West. Now the tide is turning again. As the West becomes apostate, revival is exploding throughout Asia and in parts of Europe. We must hear the cry of the psalmist: "The wicked shall be turned into hell, and all the nations that forget God" (Psalm 9:17).

The greatest danger, however, may be the polluting of our Judeo-Christian doctrines and values by the insertion or incorporation of New Age ideology. We must base our doctrines on the infallible Word of God. The admonition to search the Scriptures means more than ever before to the sincere Christian. Everything we hear or see must be weighed for accuracy and measured against the Word of God.

False teachers abound in these last days as Christ said they would (Matthew 24:4, 5). One of Paul's sternest warnings to last-day Christians was to beware of false teachers who would teach "doctrines of devils" while "speaking lies in hypocrisy" (1 Timothy 4:1, 2). Christ told a group on one occasion (and this group boasted of its religiosity), "Ye do err, not knowing the scriptures" (Matthew 22:29).

We must not believe everything we hear but "try the spirits whether they are of God" (1 John 4:1). Some cloaked in the robes of Christianity have departed from the way of truth and are teaching error. In order for discernment to operate in the church, it must work through individuals. The discerning of spirits is a gift of the Spirit. God has placed this gift in the church to profit the body of Christ (1 Corinthians 12:7, 10). When wickedness and false teaching, regardless of the robe it wears, enters the body and is not discerned until confusion and hurt have followed, then we who are supposed to be spiritual have not prayed and coveted the gifts that are available to profit the body.

We have also been warned by the Bible that Satan would try to transplant "wolves" into the church, "not sparing the flock" (Acts 20:28-30). We whom God has made shepherds have an awesome responsibility to guard God's flock jealously against such wolves (v. 28). No matter how attractive a teaching is, and no matter what it promises, if it is not based on Scripture, those who teach such a doctrine, along with their false doctrine are to be accursed (Galatians 1:8, 9). "God is not the author of confusion, but of peace, as in all churches of the saints" (1 Corinthians 14:33).

The New Age movement, with its satanic prophets and propagators, has had its highs and lows in history. Its colors and hues have changed and its dogmas have tossed to and fro, but the Word of God has remained unchanged throughout history. We take comfort and strength in the words of the prophet Isaiah: "The grass withereth, the flower fadeth: but the word of our God shall stand for ever" (Isaiah 40:8).

CHAPTER 2

SECULAR HUMANISM: THE DEATH OF HUMANITY

As we broaden our understanding of the spiritual warfare now taking place and gaining in intensity, one fact is clear: modern man is possessed with himself and his possibilities. The Scripture indicates this will be a prominent characteristic in last-day men: "This know also, that in the last days perilous times shall come. For men shall be lovers of their own selves" (2 Timothy 3:1, 2).

There is much narcissism in the world today. Narcissism is an abnormal tendency to admire one's own perfections. The term originally came from Greek mythology. A handsome youth named Narcissus saw his reflection in a pool one day and fell hopelessly in love with his beautiful face. As he gazed in fascination, he was unable to remove himself from his image and gradually pined away, staring at himself until he died.

As foolish as this mythological story seems, an overwhelming spirit of selfishness prevails among men today. Everyone wants to take care of number one. A close examination will find selfishness may be the main social disease inflicting modern society. What is behind most crimes? The answer is selfishness. Thieves steal to better their lot in life. Individuals take drugs to escape reality and enjoy the chemically induced high. Drugs are sold in order for the dealer and his kingpin to become richer. Murders are committed to satisfy motives of revenge, jealousy, hatred, or elimination. Fulfilling the lusts of the flesh satisfies the cravings of emotionally hungry and selfish individuals. No wonder Christ declared the cardinal rule of discipleship to be "If any man will come after me, let him deny himself, and take up his cross, and follow me" (Matthew 16:24).

Secular humanism is a godless philosophy that elevates the human being and centers on the worth of self. Selfishness is not compatible with the Christian life, for a life lived for Christ is one that emulates Jesus, and a selfish person is nothing at all like Jesus. Christians find it more blessed to give than receive. We pray for those who despitefully use us and go the extra mile instead of only what is asked of us. It is important to realize in the beginning that secular humanism is totally contrary to Christianity and the selfless, sacrificial, giving, and caring life.

Much has been said about the rise and influence of secular humanism during the 20th century, but very few people understand the concept, motives, and game plan of those who have devoted themselves to the spread of this ideology.

First, there are two types of humanism. The first type, generally known as *theistic humanism*, holds to a belief in the centrality of God in all things. The ancient Greeks' ideas of the rationalization of everything, along

SECULAR HUMANISM: THE DEATH OF HUMANITY

with an intertwining of Judeo-Christian thinking, became part of the basis for the theistic humanism prominent in Catholic and Anglican thought.

The second type of humanism, which is much more dangerous and influential, is man-centered *secular humanism*. Man is viewed simply as a part of nature, and the human soul is considered nonexistent. Secular humanism embraces the evolutionary teachings of Darwin and the ideas of the ancient Greek philosopher Protagoras, who taught that nothing is absolutely good or bad or true or false, and therefore each individual is his own final authority. His famous dictum was "Man is the measure of all things." Secular humanism has man replacing God and becoming the architect of his future.

Modern organized secular humanism has produced two documents of note that have laid the foundation for their conquest of the human population of earth. Two *Humanist Manifestos*, published in 1933 and 1973, spell out many of the goals and aims of this bizarre belief.

Authors Kurtz and Wilson, writing in a humanist publication, said: "The humanist still believes that traditional theism, especially faith in a prayer-hearing God, assumed to love and care for persons, to hear and understand their prayers, and to be able to do something about them, is an unproved and outmoded faith. Salvationism, based on mere affirmation, still appears as harmful, diverting people with false hopes of heaven hereafter. Reasonable minds look to other means of survival."[1]

This false intellectual movement—embraced by millions of educators, political leaders, media personnel, and youth leaders—is poisoning our society. It is godless, to say the least! Their tactic seems to be a constant

39

chipping away of the foundations of all that is good and scriptural rather than trying to overwhelm with massive revolution. God is taken out of public-school textbooks as well as references to biblical morality, ethics, and basic values. God is then replaced with evolutionary teaching. The humanists' goal of getting everyone to believe they are just the highest evolutionary animal in the biological chain is being reached by ever-increasing degrees. Morality is erased and the lie of situational ethics becomes the dogma of the day. There are no standards with the humanist—everyone does what is best for the individual.

This type of thinking seems to permeate the very fabric of modern society. But there is more here than permeation—there is propagation. The thinking of secular humanism, with all its godlessness, is the thinking of positions that matter as far as the development of future generations is concerned. Education, media, and political leadership seem its biggest converts. And why not? If the devil can control what people learn as children, what they look at and listen to as individuals, and who guides and directs their everyday living, then he has control of them.

The Bible is replete with examples of men and women who felt they had the power within themselves to make the world become what they wanted even if it meant defying God himself.

Nebuchadnezzar, the great ruler of Babylon, had seen many great accomplishments realized during his reign. According to the Bible, known or unknown to himself, he had become an instrument of judgment which God used to turn backslidden nations back to Himself (Jeremiah 29:21; 43:10; Ezekiel 29:19; 30:24). Nebuchadnezzar's home, the city of Babylon, was a marvel of engineering and beautiful splendor. The

SECULAR HUMANISM: THE DEATH OF HUMANITY

city's walls were so thick four horse-driven chariots could drive side by side atop them. A deep moat and a tremendous army guaranteed the city's safety. The hanging gardens that decorated the palace of Nebuchadnezzar was a wonder of the ancient world. The city and empire bustled with trade and commerce, and gold flowed as if liquefied into the coffers of the inhabitants. In Babylon the arts and literature flourished, and the city's science and education were unequaled in the world of its day.

In Daniel 4 we are told a remarkable story. One day as Nebuchadnezzar mused on the city of Babylon and the proud empire it represented, he declared a belief so humanistic it could be a speech to modern American secular humanists in a hotel convention hall somewhere: "Is not this great Babylon, that I have built for the house of the kingdom by the might of my power, and for the honour of my majesty?" (v. 30).

According to the Bible, "while the word was in the king's mouth" (v. 31), God pronounced judgment on him. He became instantly, within the hour, insane. He would remain so for seven years. He became as an animal and ate grass and slept in the wild. His hair and nails grew long like that of an animal. His condition was an extremely rare one that does exist in the annals of medical science. It is called *lycanthropy* and comes from the Greek word *lykos*, meaning "wolf," and the word *anthropos*, meaning "man." In the throes of the disease the person imagines himself to be an animal of some sort and refuses all hygiene and care. The ancients would drive such people from human dwellings, fearing that it was a contagious condition. According to the Bible, Nebuchadnezzar was completely cured after seven years when he acknowledged the true God of heaven and gave Him due praise.

Jezebel, wife of Ahab (king of Israel), and daughter of Ethbaal (king of the Zidonians), was another person possessed with self. She slew God's prophets, killed the innocent to obtain land deeds, and instituted a religion of idol worship that involved prostitution and sexual perversions. She slew innocent children and had them sacrificed to her idol gods, roasting some alive in the fire. Her disregard for the sanctity of life reminds one of the disregard of life characteristic of the pro-abortion forces of secular humanism today. Jezebel would not be cured. She died at the hands of her servants beneath the chariot wheels of a zealous servant of God in fulfillment of a prophecy God gave to Elijah.

When human beings deem themselves as right and perfect and the sum of their total existence, they are on the road to secular humanism. They soon see no need for God. The teaching of evolution in modern times promotes this philosophy, and it becomes the mind-set of those who embrace it. Convinced they are the highest epitome of development in the evolutionary process, God and His laws are ruled out of their life. They don't believe in Creation, so to them the entire Bible holds no truth. It is only interesting literature and a standard of ethics you can choose to live by or disregard.

Why is secular humanism something that must be considered in spiritual warfare? Simply put, it is the underlying philosophy behind much of modern thinking. Secular humanism says there is no God to hear, be responsible to, read about, or believe in. Christians are labeled as fools, fanatics, and extremists. What you have here is a spirit of antichrist. It comes from our old antagonists and, sadly, it is the spirit of much of the young and educated world today. The people that will form the leadership of tomorrow are enlisting by the thousands into the ranks of secular humanism.

SECULAR HUMANISM: THE DEATH OF HUMANITY

We are not wrestling with flesh and blood. We are fighting in the spiritual realms of heinous darkness, and we must have divine assistance.

We are seeing what few generations have ever witnessed. We are seeing the changing of a culture. We are going from a Judeo-Christian culture to a culture of secular humanism based on Darwinistic evolution and worship of the creature instead of the Creator.

Is there hope? Is there a solution? Can an answer be found? Yes, a thousand times yes! We, as born-again, redeemed Christians, must take control of our lives and those of our children and grandchildren. This war is not an educational war, nor is it a war with Hollywood or Madison Avenue, nor are we skirmishing with the political hacks who run the palaces of power. Our warfare is spiritual, not carnal. We are dealing with a very real devil who leads legions of very real demons. He and his entire host are intelligent, articulate, knowledgeable of human ways, and subtle in their craftiness. And they hold much of the earth's population in their sway.

We must come to grips with the reality of the existence of secular humanism as a tool of evil. Then we can organize and carry out our strategy.

Our foundation is hope, and we have no reason to be embarrassed about that, for the Scripture says, "And hope maketh not ashamed; because the love of God is shed abroad in our hearts by the Holy Ghost which is given unto us" (Romans 5:5). Our hope is based on the Bible as the only true, lasting testimony of real truth (Isaiah 40:8; John 17:17; 2 Peter 1:20, 21).

We must, then, counteract our Enemy's tactics by teaching, preaching, and telling the truth of the Word of God concerning the human condition. Men must know "all have sinned, and come short of the glory of God"

43

(Romans 3:23). They must be told "the heart is deceitful above all things, and desperately wicked" (Jeremiah 17:9).

In other words, we need the old-fashioned preaching of the gospel of salvation in its power and purity. Only salvation can change the human condition. Secular humanism offers no hope beyond the grave. Only Christ can bring hope and peace. We must never underestimate the power of the gospel. The world is hungry for truth. No matter how callous they are, when people look at themselves and the creation surrounding them, the image of God within them recognizes God is there somewhere. They may never admit it and they may often deny it, but the seed of truth is in their hearts. We must never forget that no one is hopeless. The Bible has declared, "For the grace of God that bringeth salvation hath appeared to all men" (Titus 2:11).

People must be told man is not the product of 2 billion years of accidental, happenstance evolution but that man was "fearfully and wonderfully made" (Psalm 139:14) "in the image of God" (Genesis 1:27).

They must be told man needs a Redeemer to save him from his sinful condition, God has provided such a Redeemer in Jesus Christ, and a plan of salvation has been given to restore man to God (John 3:16, 17).

In short, the body of Christ must get back into the Word. We must read it, memorize it, teach it, proclaim it, live it, and interpret it, using it as the criterion of interpretation. This is a simple truth, but it is profound and powerful. Jesus said it best: "And ye shall know the truth, and the truth shall make you free" (John 8:32).

We don't have to rely on intellectual arguments to validate our position. Our reasons are those of faith and good sense. We are ready to give to every man an

SECULAR HUMANISM: THE DEATH OF HUMANITY

answer for the hope that lies within us. With the song-writer we sing:

> My hope is built on nothing less
> Than Jesus' blood and righteousness;
> I dare not trust the sweetest frame,
> But wholly lean on Jesus' name.
> On Christ, the solid Rock, I stand;
> All other ground is sinking sand,
> All other ground is sinking sand.

Some say that preaching or proclamation will not work. Paul did much of his ministry in the Greek world, which had been mesmerized by philosophy and bizarre myths and tales of fantasy from the so-called gods and goddesses of Mount Olympus that had ruled the thinking of the people from their infancy. But Paul was emphatic in what he knew was God's method to win the secular humanists and occultists of his day. He stated in 1 Corinthians 1:21: "For after that in the wisdom of God the world by wisdom knew not God, it pleased God by the foolishness of preaching to save them that believe."

Faith comes by hearing, and hearing by the Word of God. But how can they hear without a preacher? And how can he preach unless he is sent? (Romans 10:14-17). Faith is a powerful seed that once implanted in the fertile ground of the heart can take root and produce salvation. God designed us to believe. Adam and Eve believed everything God said about the Garden of Eden and the Tree of Knowledge of Good and Evil. It was the devil's lie that deceived Eve. The Word of God is unlike other books, for it comes from God himself. Once planted, it never returns to God void, but He sends it forth to accomplish His divine purposes (Isaiah 55:11).

God's method is the Word. His method, put in

SPIRIT WARS

practice, will work. The Book of Jeremiah says it best: "Is not my word like as a fire? saith the Lord; and like a hammer that breaketh the rock in pieces?" (23:29).

The philosophy from hell known as secular humanism will bring death to its adherents. Some who follow its false teachings harden themselves like granite against the truth of salvation. But Jeremiah the prophet said it doesn't matter. God's Word breaks all rocks of resistance in pieces and truth prevails. Listen to the words of Christ Jesus: "Ye shall know the truth, and the truth shall make you free" (John 8:32).

Endnote

[1]Ian T. Taylor, *In the Minds of Men* (Toronto: TFE Publishing, 1987), pp. 420, 421.

CHAPTER 3

THE OCCULT: WICKEDNESS IN HIGH PLACES

It is important to know there are many dangers involved in the study and recognition of the occult. Perhaps the greatest danger is in sensationalizing this movement and its power, especially its effect on Christianity. Though we should heed the advice of the apostle Paul and not be ignorant of Satan's devices (2 Corinthians 2:11), we also should remember "God hath not given us the spirit of fear; but of power, and of love, and of a sound mind" (2 Timothy 1:7).

In a definitive study of satanism and the occult, there is a tendency to study the surface symbols of this horror and overlook the subtle intents and purposes of this evil movement. The human imagination, especially among the young, is fascinated with goat heads, pentagrams, Ouija boards, incantations, warlocks, witches, white and black magic, secret societies, necromancy, and a vast host of paraphernalia and satanic objects.

SPIRIT WARS

All of these things are involved in the occult, but behind them is the true intent of Lucifer, the prince of the power of the air. The distant thunder of the Antichrist storm that will sweep the world is coming closer. Communication with, and acceptance by, the world is the one goal Satanists are striving for and achieving. Their influence shows in many elements of modern society. Hollywood, the world of fictionalized literature, role-playing games, video games, and modern music are targets for satanic takeover. These appeal to people's worldly lusts. "For all that is in the world, the lust of the flesh, and the lust of the eyes, and the pride of life, is not of the Father, but is of the world" (1 John 2:16). By influencing what people see, hear, and turn to for entertainment, Satanists are gaining a tolerance not possible before the coming of mass media.

Occult representatives and leaders have been invited to conventions and symposiums involving religious leaders from a broad spectrum of American life. The fact that they were invited, along with their very presence, states that their opinions and ideology, though bizarre, were considered mainstream enough to be valued. Here we see a violation of the very foundational teachings of Christ, who emphatically stated, "No servant can serve two masters: for either he will hate the one, and love the other; or else he will hold to the one, and despise the other" (Luke 16:13). The apostle Paul strongly reiterated this when he asked the Corinthian church, "What fellowship hath righteousness with unrighteousness? and what communion hath light with darkness? And what concord hath Christ with Belial? or what part hath he that believeth with an infidel? And what agreement hath the temple of God with idols?" (2 Corinthians 6:14-16).

Let us attempt to gain a definitive understanding of

THE OCCULT: WICKEDNESS IN HIGH PLACES

the occult and the modern Satanist movement. The reader should be cautioned this subject could be defined by volumes, so our intent is to gain an understanding of basic terms as we prepare to do spiritual warfare with the oldest of enemies.

To come to an understanding, it is important that we deal with the occult and satanism as two separate entities, though they are interrelated with each other.

The study of the occult is usually classified into three separate arenas of interest: spiritism, fortune-telling, and magic. These, as we shall see, are strictly forbidden by Scripture.

Spiritism, according to Dr. Michael Green in his book *Exposing the Prince of Darkness,* is the attempt to communicate with the spirits of the dead. He states, "Whether this is, in fact, achieved, or whether people are put in touch with demonic forces masquerading as the spirits of the dead, is, for the moment, irrelevant. The point is that whereas much is chicanery and trickery in this area of the occult, as in others, much is not. Through trances, through seances, through mediums and Ouija boards, table-turning and the like, messages from 'the other side' are often received. To be sure, they are usually trivial or banal, but it cannot be denied that, time and again, they do put men and women in touch with the spirit world."[1]

This is strictly forbidden in the Word of God. In Deuteronomy 18:9-12, God told Israel, "When thou art come into the land which the Lord thy God giveth thee, thou shalt not learn to do after the abominations of those nations. There shall not be found among you any one that maketh his son or his daughter to pass through the fire, or that useth divination, or an observer of times, or an enchanter, or a witch, or a charmer, or a consulter with familiar spirits, or a wizard, or a

49

SPIRIT WARS

necromancer. For all that do these things are an abomination unto the Lord: and because of these abominations the Lord thy God doth drive them out from before thee."

Notice that God forbids all elements of the occult—spiritism, fortune-telling, and magic practitioners. Notice, also, in Deuteronomy 18:12, how God has the power to "drive them out." No occult power that has existed in the history of the universe is the equal in battle to God and His servants.

Fortune-telling involves divination, which is the attempt to foretell and explore the future. This includes palmistry, tarot cards, horoscopes, crystal balls, card laying, numerology, and psychometry (the ability to tell someone's fortune by holding an object belonging to that person). In Acts 16, Paul and Silas found a young damsel possessed with a spirit of divination who was bringing her masters much gain with her demonic fortune-telling ability. Paul prayed for her deliverance, and she was set free from that spirit (v. 18). The Scripture is emphatic in its declaration that Satan is "a liar, and the father of it" (John 8:44). Therefore, his children are liars, and those in his servitude cannot be counted on to tell the truth about the future even if they could determine it or control it—which they cannot. Those who delve into divination and fortune-telling open themselves to demonic influence and possession and control by evil spirits. They become soldiers, knowingly or unknowingly, in Satan's subtle scheme to overcome righteousness. Their fortune, unless they find redemption, has been told, and it is a true report: "They which do such things shall not inherit the kingdom of God" (Galatians 5:21).

Magic, simply put, is the ability to control, change, or manipulate nature, circumstances, and the environment

THE OCCULT: WICKEDNESS IN HIGH PLACES

to serve some particular purpose or end. Scripture forbids it (Deuteronomy 18:11; Galatians 5:20). Satan's limited power allows it to exist, but it can never overcome or overrule the power of the living God. The Scripture plainly declares, "Greater is he that is in you, than he that is in the world" (1 John 4:4).

There is, of course, the business of slight of hand or trickery practiced by magicians, who, when going to extremes, dabble with the occult. But magic in the occult sense is much more bizarre and sinister. Black magic, incantations, voodoo, spells, curses, and sacrificial offerings of blood and flesh all are a part of the magic of the occult. It is evidently spurred on by demonic powers.

Are there results? Certainly; evil things have happened as the result of demonic activity among the unrighteous. Demon worshipers in South Africa worship a demon who has the power to stop the flow of blood. They place grotesque, huge hooks through their flesh and attach ropes with which to pull the demon's temple on a cart through the streets. Satanic priests in Indonesia have, under magic spells, been reported to jump over houses. I have seen an unretouched film, taken by a Pentecostal missionary, of a satanic priest blowing streams of fire from his mouth six to eight feet long.

These demonstrations, in underdeveloped countries, serve to inspire fear in the people who follow these sinister forces. In Western culture there is a tendency to scoff and look down on these demonstrations of paganism. However, is our culture any less pagan with its fixation on science fiction and its fascination with video fantasy? While the world starves for bread, we spend billions on genetic engineering, cloning, and the possibilities that we might produce electronic holograms

51

where a person's fantasies of any nature can be realized. Escapism from reality and from God's purpose for man on this earth, which is to glorify Him, takes many forms. The poor ragged peasant of a Third World country and the Manhattan businessman in a custom-tailored suit are the same in the sight of God. Romans 3:23 is not a joke: "All have sinned, and come short of the glory of God."

The occult is taking prisoners from every element of society in every segment of the globe. Minds are being conditioned so that men will willingly accept the promises of hope and peace made by the Antichrist. In Revelation 6:2 he is seen riding the white horse of peace, but in verse 8 the horse of death is his mount, and hell follows him.

The only hope for those who are involved in the occult is to turn to Christ with all their heart. The great hope of all, no matter how enslaved they are, is still 1 John 1:9: "If we confess our sins, he is faithful and just to forgive us our sins, and to cleanse us from all unrighteousness."

Satanism, with its myriad of directions, is a subject the devil wants the weak and unsuspecting to delve into; but he absolutely does not want a born-again, blood-washed, Spirit-filled child of God to have a working knowledge of what his fiendish following is all about.

According to George Mather and Larry Nichols, in their excellent work *Dictionary of Cults, Sects, Religions and the Occult*, there are five basic categories of Satanists that can be divided into two categories—Group Satanists and Individual Satanists.[2] Under *Group Satanists* there are four divisions:

1. *Traditional.* Their chief characteristics are that they are secretive, have an intense hatred for Christianity,

THE OCCULT: WICKEDNESS IN HIGH PLACES

celebrate the Black Mass (including the use of the communion cup of blood), and strongly believe Satan exists.

2. *Nontraditional.* They are very secretive, have a hatred for Christianity born out of non-Christian philosophy such as Eastern mysticism, they drink blood—not to emulate the communion but rather look upon it as a life source—and they believe Satan exists.

3. *Public Satanists.* They are nonsecretive, hold worship services in public, base their teachings on Anton LaVey's *Satanic Bible,* and they believe Satan is a force or symbol of evil.

4. *Youth Gang Satanists.* These are not avowed Satanists but "dabblers" in the occult through the influence of drugs and heavy-metal music. They look upon satanism as a symbol of rebellion against authority, and to many of them it is a passing fad. Most have little knowledge of true satanism, and they may not believe Satan exists.

The second category, *Individual Satanists,* has only one division. These people are not members of any group but are highly individualized and have many bizarre beliefs. Often they are disturbed neurotic/psychotic individuals. Many atrocious crimes have been perpetrated by these people who obviously are under a demonic grip and possession.

The influence of Satanists today may often be overstated. While they do have a dominating influence on such things as the media, rock music, the drug culture, and other theaters of evil, they do not constitute a majority of the population but are still a very small minority. But they are growing in number, and it is with this realization that Christians need to take a sober look at what is happening.

An article in the June 1993 issue of *Vanity Fair* dealt

53

with people who make claims of horrifying satanic cult and ritual abuse that allegedly occurred during their childhood.[3] Mental health and law enforcement professionals are baffled and divided over this modern phenomenon.

Many believe these memories are false, the product of mass hysteria and sensationalized tabloid television. Nevertheless, there are those who cite the accuracy of these memories, many of which have been verified through hypnosis and the use of sodium pentothal.

There is enough evidence in the files of the FBI and others indicating that satanic cults have been responsible for human sacrifices, child disappearances, bizarre sexual-abuse cases, and human mutilation in cult ceremonies to cause great concern by us all. There must be demonic work involved in these satanic rituals.

In the *Vanity Fair* article a victim described how as a young teenager she was raped by her father and grandfather, as well as other members of a satanic cult, and impregnated repeatedly only to have premature labor artificially induced in a barnyard ceremony and the aborted fetus then sacrificed to Satan by the cult. Herein lies demonic work of the basest sort: murder—foul and purposeful. Other claims of an even more horrible nature have been made concerning Satanists and their evil rituals.

What could possess human beings to become so vile? Only demons—the fallen angels of Lucifer's hellish horde—could fill people's minds with such atrocities. And yet, one is made to wonder what causes an entire nation and its sophisticated politicians, lawyers, judges, and medical personnel to wink and turn their head at the murder of over 30 million unborn children in the abortion mills of this country.

THE OCCULT: WICKEDNESS IN HIGH PLACES

Is not the same Satan and his evil host at work? The innocent are slain today through abortion just as surely as they were when Pharaoh slew Hebrew babies in the days of Moses, and just as Herod butchered the babies of Bethlehem after the birth of Jesus. Satan, like a chameleon, may change his colors and cloak, but his evil purposes remain the same.

Much rumor and innuendo have been stated of late about the intent of Satanists toward the church. Many cite the vast number of moral failures among the clergy and the apathy and demise of many Evangelical churches as the work of conspiring Satanists. Is this true? This poses some questions that must be addressed from a biblical standpoint.

First, it is true that Satan is at war with the saints. This war began in the splendor of Eden's garden many years ago. Satan fired the first shots and Adam and Eve fell dead in their trespasses and sins. Our first ancestors were casualties of satanic attack, and the original sin occurred. The war has never ceased. Tactics may change and devices may increase, but the devil is still attacking.

It is entirely possible that Satan's devotees pray to him for the downfall of Christianity. There have been too many reports of "satanic plants," feigning Christianity, entering churches for the sole purpose of disruption. Stories abound of seducers and seductresses who appear on the scene to tempt and allure and cause the downfall of clergy and laity alike within the church world. A Pentecostal pastor in the western United States reported that his church was suddenly, within weeks, filled with new people, who, after establishing themselves, began to practice ritualistic religious practices and worship that went far beyond the norm. When confronted, they confessed they had come

55

purposely to take over and that their group was basically New Age/Satanist, led by a witch and warlock.

Other pastors, in various regions of the United States and Europe, report vandalism, theft, arson, and blasphemy of their church facilities, with Satanists openly taking credit for the destruction. A pastor in the southeastern United States was told by the police, after they had apprehended the suspects, that they confessed they had to desecrate a church to be accepted into a satanic coven. And desecrate they did—writing vulgarisms in red paint, defecating on the altars, and making general destruction of the facilities.

The tragedy is that we in Christianity, especially we Evangelicals who believe in the power of the blood of Christ and the Spirit of God, are not on the offensive against the devil. Whatever we "bind on earth shall be bound in heaven" (Matthew 16:19); our weapons are "mighty through God to the pulling down of strong holds" (2 Corinthians 10:4); "Greater is he that is in you, than he that is in the world" (1 John 4:4); "God hath not given us the spirit of fear" (2 Timothy 1:7); and we have been promised that when hell and all its forces amass themselves against the church of the living God, they "shall not prevail against it" (Matthew 16:18), for "the Spirit of the Lord shall lift up a standard against [them]" (Isaiah 59:19).

Why, then, is there a falling away? Why would men and women through whom the Spirit of the living God has flowed and who have been instruments of His power fall to the tempter?

One only has to look into biblical history to see the weakness of humanity against the Evil One when those humans tried to fight Satan by their own strength. In every instance, those who fell were not where they should have been spiritually.

THE OCCULT: WICKEDNESS IN HIGH PLACES

Instead of leading the battle, David gave the command to Joab and was lounging on his roof when he spied Bathsheba bathing and his lust consumed him (2 Samuel 11:1-5).

Demas, who had been the faithful servant of the apostle Paul, forsook the ministry, and the Bible's sad commentary is "Demas hath forsaken me, having loved this present world" (2 Timothy 4:10).

The city of Jericho and its idolatrous contents were forbidden by God to Israel, for God said they were accursed (Joshua 6:17, 18). Jericho had become a satanic city, and its paraphernalia and riches, if taken, would contaminate the holy people of God. Achan, the son of Carmi, should have stayed away from this accursed fallen city, but he partook of the accursed things and died in horrible judgment (7:24, 25).

Abner, the son of Ner, lived safely in Hebron, the city of refuge. Joab, a wicked killer, wanted his life but could not have it, for Abner was in a place of refuge. But Abner wandered near the gate. Joab, waiting at the gate, lured him out and stabbed him to death (2 Samuel 3:27). His departure from the city of refuge was his departure from protection.

Sound biblical sense and thinking is the preservative that modern Christianity needs so desperately. We must get back into reading, studying, and committing to memory God's Word.

Christ in us is the "hope of glory" (Colossians 1:27). We do not have to fear Satan or his evil forces. Our hope is in God, who made heaven and earth (Psalm 146:5, 6). We must cling to the Cross and give ourselves to prayer, fasting, and reading and proclaiming the Word.

There are two things we need especially to watch pertaining to the occult:

SPIRIT WARS

First, we need to be watchful for increasing Satanist activity in the areas of church infiltration and deception. I would not become paranoid concerning this, but there have been enough reports and rumors in the Evangelical world concerning "satanic disrupters" that we must not take it lightly. Besides this, we have been given several biblical warnings about just such possibilities taking place. In Jude's epistle he states concerning the faith: "It is in danger from certain persons who have wormed their way in, the very men whom Scripture long ago marked down for the doom they have incurred. They are the enemies of religion; they pervert the free favour of our God into licentiousness, disowning Jesus Christ, our only Master and Lord" (Jude 4, NEB). The apostle Peter said of these "false teachers" and infiltrators that they would "bring in damnable heresies . . . denying the Lord that bought them" (2 Peter 2:1). He also said they "walk after the flesh in the lust of uncleanness, and despise government. Presumptuous are they, selfwilled, they are not afraid to speak evil of dignities" (v. 10).

I believe Satan is attacking the church through his followers. I do not believe they will enjoy any permanent victories nor long-term success. In fact, as Peter said in verse 1, they will "bring upon themselves swift destruction." But I believe only the church that is in tune with heaven, seasoned with prayer, and wearing God's armor will experience victory. Churches that are prayerless, carnal, self-centered, finding fault with each other, and weak in the Word will see some decimation of the flock by these wolves. We must build a wall of prayer and Holy Ghost power around our congregations.

The second thing we must do is guard our homes from satanic attack. In the Old Testament it was the

58

THE OCCULT: WICKEDNESS IN HIGH PLACES

responsibility of the Jewish father to keep his home free of idols and pagan influence. As the priest of his home, he fulfilled this responsibility to keep his home a sacred place where the blessings of God could abound toward him and his family.

There has been a subtle infiltration of satanic things into homes throughout our society. Guard what your children watch on television. Many cartoons are demonic and have satanic overtones. Hard-rock music such as is seen on MTV is full of satanic symbols and worship. Many toys, comic books, and science-fiction literature are full of the trappings of the occult.

A noted Pentecostal pastor told of a time when his immediate family constantly had had a sick family member or one accident or disaster after another for weeks and months. To top it all, it seemed a spirit of depression accompanied these events. After prayer he felt led of God to search and cleanse his home of any unclean thing. He finally found a painting bought on a foreign-missions trip that had cleverly hidden satanic symbols in the scenery. Upon the destruction of the painting, all satanic oppression ceased. You might ask, Can this really be possible? The answer is in a question: Does Satan exist? Of course he does, and he lives to make war on the saints. He doesn't have dominance, but he has certain parameters allowed. In this case, a godly man was drawn to prayer, and through prayer he made a spiritual discovery that led to the removal of Satan's influence and caused his defeat. Never forget that Satan was allowed within the parameters of Job's life for Job's testing.

While it is important to keep our guard up and remain in spiritual fighting condition, we need to understand that we must not become overoccupied with Satan observing. We counteract evil's influence with the good found in Christ. Paul tells us plainly what we are to do:

"Finally, brethren, whatsoever things are true, whatsoever things are honest, whatsoever things are just, whatsoever things are pure, whatsoever things are lovely, whatsoever things are of good report; if there be any virtue, and if there be any praise, think on these things" (Philippians 4:8).

Endnotes

[1]Michael Green, *Exposing the Prince of Darkness* (Ann Arbor: Servant Publications, 1991), p. 120.

[2]George A. Mather and Larry A. Nichols, *Dictionary of Cults, Sects, Religions and the Occult* (Grand Rapids: Zondervan Publishing House, 1993), p. 245.

[3]Leslie Bennetts, "Nightmares on Main Street," *Vanity Fair*, June 1993, p. 42.

CHAPTER 4

SCIENCE FALSELY SO CALLED

Writing to the young minister Timothy, Paul warned him to avoid "profane and vain babblings and . . . science falsely so called: which some professing have erred concerning the faith" (1 Timothy 6:20, 21).

Perhaps nothing has shaped the thinking of modern people and drawn them away from the living God like the teaching of evolution—not as a theory but as a scientific fact. The teaching of evolutionary science is one of the most subtle and powerful tactics ever used by the devil in spiritual warfare.

When Charles Darwin published *On the Origin of Species* in 1859, little did he realize the impact it would have upon humanity. Though the word *evolution* did not appear until the sixth printing in 1872, the book caused an immediate uproar upon its first release. Newspapers denounced it, and pulpits throughout Christendom fervently warned of its potential danger.

SPIRIT WARS

In 1871 Darwin published another work, titled *The Descent of Man and Selection in Relation to Sex.* In it he said: "Man is descended from a hairy-tailed quadruped . . . an inhabitant of the Old World . . . the progenitor of the . . . New World monkeys." Public dissent of this book was limited, perhaps because so much energy had been expended in protesting *Origins*, suggests Ian Taylor in his book *In the Minds of Men.*

In 1872 Darwin published *The Expression of the Emotions in Men and Animals.* In this book he noted the similarities of men and animals in expressing anger, happiness, violence, and other emotions. Because of this work many psychologists consider Darwin to be the father of Freudian psychology.

Though Darwin may be the creator of the modern evolutionary movement, a figure far more sinister than Charles Darwin is behind this. Satan, the great deceiver, is behind much of the false science of today. And once again his main tactic is to question the validity of God's Word as he did in the Garden of Eden.

Evolution teaches that man ascended from lower forms of life. It teaches that from single-celled life forms grew multicelled and multifaceted creatures; and through mutations, chemical changes, and environmental conditions, life evolved into many different species, all akin to each other, with man being the highest-ascended form of the primate. Some in religious circles have tried to adapt this theory to the Creation passages in Genesis saying, in effect, God used evolution to accomplish His total creation. But why would an omniscient and omnipotent God resort to using such an inefficient and cruel process? The Bible plainly declares that what God did at Creation was "very good" (Genesis 1:31).

The teaching of evolution is totally contrary to

62

SCIENCE FALSELY SO CALLED

Scripture. In the Genesis account of Creation, God made everything "after his kind," meaning that each species of plant and animal was unique and created individually by God. However, a generation of people around the world has grown up believing they are a highly evolved animal species.

People who believe they are advanced animals quickly make some dangerous deductions. They know animals are not bound by morals, laws, and limits of behavior—other than physical ones—for their order is determined only by natural boundaries. The evolutionary view allows man the same freedom from responsibility.

This thinking resulted in the sexual revolution of the late 20th century, which ushered in a wave of unbridled moral decay and escalating violence on a scale like the world has not seen since the days of Noah before the Flood.

Belief in evolution makes a mockery of great Christian doctrines like the fall of man and the need of a Redeemer, life after death, eternity in heaven or hell, and the need of the church on the earth. Evolutionary thinking is ushering in the spirit of antichrist, which John said comes from the spirit that teaches Jesus Christ has not come in the flesh (1 John 4:3). In other words, this spirit says there is no need of a Redeemer since man has not fallen but is slowly evolving upward.

The great laws of free nations are based on the Word of God. The Scripture is plain: "Blessed is the nation whose God is the Lord" (Psalm 33:12). On the other hand, humanism, which has as its foundation the teaching of evolution, gripped Europe in the early years of the 20th century, and the resulting rise of fascism, Nazism, communism, widespread perversion, and a casual acceptance of immorality brought spiritual destruction throughout the continent.

In America this heinous teaching, accompanied by the forbidding of prayer and the reading of God's Word, is creating a nation filled with people who have no hope and live in despair. An unparalleled rise of random violence, a plague of pornography and promiscuity, an epidemic of sexually transmitted diseases, and a grip of materialistic greed are all hallmarks of a generation that looks upon an orangutan as a distant cousin. Evolution offers a hopeless morass of misery. It is a lie, and lies have only one source—the father of liars, the devil himself.

The truth is, the Bible is exactly right. Humankind was made in the image of God (Genesis 1:27). Man needs God, for though he fell in the original sin, he retains part of the nature of God in him. For man to be restored to fellowship, he still needs a Redeemer that will pay the punishment for his sinful condition and restore him back to a right relationship with God. Because man is made in the image of God, he has within him Godlike attributes—such as morality, creativity, artistry, intelligent reasoning ability, a capacity to love and cherish, the ability to forgive and be kind—and he loves to give and receive praise. Yet man is not God, nor will he ever become God, as the serpent taught in Genesis 3 and the New Age serpents of our day are teaching.

Man is God's creation. Redeemed men and women become children of God, and God can then equip them for service to help His kingdom on earth.

Many notable born-again scientists call themselves "Creation scientists." These godly men and women have scientific degrees and credentials of experience, yet they believe the Bible is the inspired Word of God

SCIENCE FALSELY SO CALLED

and they accept and teach the Genesis account of Creation. Many of them have debated noted evolutionists and stood tall and scientific for biblical truth. They give a good account of themselves and boldly defend the gospel. Theirs is a very special spiritual warfare. They are contending for the minds of precious youth, and they sincerely want the young people to accept the truth as found in the Scripture.

Evangelical Christendom needs to pray for Christian professors, teachers, and scientists who believe in the biblical account of Creation, that they may walk in the power of the Spirit and proclaim the truth in their special way. These scientists have become convinced through study that the Bible makes more scientific sense than Darwinism. Intricate patterns, precise design, similarities in life forms, continuance of species, and thousands of other wonders speak of a divine and loving Creator.

False science that lies about man's origins and has Satan for its chief scientist has filled our world with misery. Only when mankind can say with the psalmist David, "I am fearfully and wonderfully made" (Psalm 139:14) and can sing "I'm redeemed by love divine" will he truly begin to serve God's purpose for him on this earth. Man was created to glorify God (Isaiah 43:7).

CHAPTER 5

DEMONS:
SATAN'S EVIL HENCHMEN

"For we wrestle not against flesh and blood, but against principalities, against powers, against the rulers of the darkness of this world, against spiritual wickedness in high places" (Ephesians 6:12).

In Paul's excellent treatise to the Ephesians on spiritual warfare, he warned them of four types of rebellious evil-spirit enemies they would contend with as they endeavored to serve Christ. In the above passage we see a powerful biblical explanation of rank, order, and organization in the demon world. The Bible does not try to prove the existence of demons; it plainly states they exist and are both intelligent and active.

Notice Paul's ranking of demonic powers. The English word *principalities* is translated from the Greek word *archas*, which means "chief rulers" or "beings of the highest rank." It only makes sense that Satan, who held a post of authority in heaven before his fall (Ezekiel 28), would adopt a governmental system to rule his dominion and carry out his plans. Therefore, he must have evil spirits in positions of rulership either geographically or in areas of satanic work.

The English word *powers* is translated from the Greek word *exousias*, which means "authorities" and refers to the fact these evil specialists derive their power from and execute the will of the chief rulers or principalities.

The word *rulers* in the English phrase *"rulers of the darkness of this world"* is translated from the Greek *kosmokratoras*, which means "the spirit-world rulers of darkness." The Bible teaches satanic government and territorial rulership among demons (Ephesians 6:12). These are demons who rule dark areas of this world both geographically and spiritually. Darkness is always opposed to light and cannot comprehend it.

The final words Paul used, *spiritual wickedness*, are translated from the Greek words *pneumatika tes ponerias*, and refer to the wicked spirits of Satan in the heavens. These are powers literally in the air, and their mission is constant warfare against God's angels and the obstruction of angelic duties. They want to thwart the work of angels in God's dealings with men.

The experience of the prophet Daniel in chapter 10 is a prime example of this. Here the prophet was told by Gabriel that an evil spirit who ruled the territory of Persia "withstood" him for three weeks. The deadlock was broken when the archangel Michael came to help Gabriel (vv. 12, 13).

When Christ was tempted in the wilderness, Satan said he would give Him "the kingdoms of the world, and the glory of them" if He would fall down and worship him (Matthew 4:8, 9). It would be easy to label this a lie, but here, as in most of Satan's lies, there is an element of truth. Though we know "the earth is the Lord's, and the fulness thereof" (Psalm 24:1), much of

DEMONS: SATAN'S EVIL HENCHMEN

the real estate or disposable things here belong to Satan. They are built for his purposes and serve his evil intentions. It is reasonable to conclude he places governors and kings of his principalities in positions of evil spiritual leadership to perpetrate his causes. These evil henchmen rule sinful areas of kingdoms and cities. Notice how many geographical areas from world-class cities to small hamlets have their sections of evil. For instance, in Amsterdam, Holland, the red-light district is labeled as such on maps of that massive metropolis. In various cities of the world are areas of commerce, pornography, bars, gambling, drug infestation, prostitution, homosexuality, and sweatshops where human slavery is still practiced. Christians visiting these areas, either as tourists or in evangelistic endeavors, often find tremendous satanic oppression. Many will tell you evil can be felt like a heavy weight bearing down upon them.

I have visited many areas of the world where authoritarian atheistic governments ruled or where idol worship or mysticism and spiritism were practiced. I have been in areas of the Caribbean where voodoo and witchcraft abounded. In these geographic locations I could sense a powerful satanic oppression. This oppression would bear down and increase when I would bow to pray, read the Word of God, or join in a Christian worship service. Another common thread in these areas where Christianity is in the minority and evil rules is abject poverty and a sense of hopelessness among the people. Unbridled lust and addictions to various drugs and alcohol are not only common but the rule rather than the exception. Surely demons rule and concentrate themselves in these places.

Another noteworthy conclusion to be drawn from Satan's boast to Christ about the kingdoms of this world being his is that he evidently exerts control and

SPIRIT WARS

influence over world governments. Three times in John's Gospel, Jesus referred to Satan as "the prince of this world" (12:31; 14:30; 16:11). The word *prince* here literally means governmental ruler. The same word is used of him in Ephesians 2:2, where Paul described him as "the prince of the power of the air." In 1 John 5:19 the apostle John tells us "the whole world lieth in wickedness." The evil system ruled by Satan is the dwelling place of the men of this earth who have alienated themselves from God. The result of Satan's influence over world governments is pronounced clearly in wars, greed, governmental dominance over church rights and practices, legalizing of abortion, immorality, and condemnation of public Christian religious practice.

Isaiah the prophet, in his panoramic passage in chapter 14 dealing with the fall of Lucifer, said Lucifer "weakened the nations" (v. 12, *NKJV*) and "made the world as a wilderness and destroyed its cities" (v. 17, *NKJV*). It is ludicrous to think Satan and his demonic henchmen have ceased in their desire to dominate and bring about the downfall of the earth. There are current territorial spirits and evil rulers, make no mistake about it. And if one poor man was possessed with a "legion" of demons (Mark 5), can you imagine the multitudes of evil ones who flood the modern populace with their influence and domination?

We need to consider the biblical limitations placed upon demons. How much power do they have? Who can they possess or oppress? Who has the power to defeat them? Can they come back once driven away?

The Bible is not cloudy concerning demons. The truth is easily understood. Again, we only want to examine biblical truth.

Demons' power is spiritual. They are created

DEMONS: SATAN'S EVIL HENCHMEN

beings—fallen angels. We know some fallen angels are "reserved in everlasting chains under darkness" (Jude 6) and there await judgment. We know some demons live in a place known as the Abyss (bottomless pit), where a demon king rules over them; his Hebrew name is Abaddon, and his Greek name is Apollyon (Revelation 9:1-11). Other demons freely operate as Satan's allies. In Matthew 25:41 we read the phrase "the devil and his angels," and in Revelation 12:7 we see the terminology "the dragon . . . and his angels." In Matthew 12:24 the devil is referred to by the Pharisees as "Beelzebub the prince of the devils."

The demons' power is at the disposal of Satan. He commands them and they use their intelligence and power to carry out his commands. Neither Satan nor any of his demons have the attributes of God. They are not omnipotent, omniscient, or omnipresent. They must operate within the boundaries God allows them. We know they cannot possess a redeemed child of God. "No man can serve two masters" (Matthew 6:24). Demons may oppress or attack a child of God even as Satan desired to "sift" Simon Peter "as wheat" (Luke 22:31), but the power of God within a Christian is much greater than any demonic power. "Greater is he that is in you, than he that is in the world" (1 John 4:4). The first four verses of 1 John 4 deal with demon spirits, but in verse 4 John emphatically states: "Ye are of God, little children, and have overcome them." The disciples returned rejoicing after Christ sent them out, saying, "Lord, even the devils are subject unto us through thy name" (Luke 10:17).

A study of the history of demon possession will verify that it most often occurs in places and among people who do not know Christ or who have rejected Him and given themselves over to satanic influence. Though

71

this horror once was found mostly in backward countries where satanic practices abounded, modern Western cultures now are seeing what can only be demon possession. A national suicide epidemic among young people, blamed on death-metal music; drug addiction; and a fascination with role-playing games like Dungeons and Dragons and Ouija boards all testify that demons are at work in Western culture.

But what about the more subtle work of demons? People who once knew Christ and have backslidden are vulnerable to possession. Some confess their backsliding; others continue to play the hypocrite. Either scenario makes the backslidden individual an obvious target. Jesus gave a fascinating and frightful account of what can happen (see Matthew 12:43-45; Luke 11:24-26). An unclean spirit who has departed from a man walks through dry places seeking rest. When he finds none, he comes back to enter the man again, bringing with him seven other evil spirits more wicked than himself. Christ said, "The last state of that man is worse than the first."

Perhaps this is the sad case of many hypocrites within the church world. Though they once served Christ as zealous newborn babes, they grew careless about their experience. They became cold and failed to pray, read the Bible, and share their faith. Church became a social institution, and they lusted for power within the framework of that institution.

Now, after a few years, they have become dominant "church bosses" running the ecclesiastical machinery of the church without love or compassion. They wink at what once convicted them and stay in a war of wits with other church leaders. They are cynical and calloused to the gospel. Their end is much worse than their beginning.

DEMONS: SATAN'S EVIL HENCHMEN

No, there are no loud, demonstrative manifestations of evil spirits in these people. Why should Satan manifest himself and his henchmen thusly? He is craftily hidden, and his hosts "despise government" and "are not afraid to speak evil of dignities" (2 Peter 2:10). Satan's victims may die full of bitterness after causing church strife and division within the body most of their lives. They backslid on a pew, and the demon and his friends entered dwellings that were "empty, swept, and garnished" (Matthew 12:44).

Let us end on a triumphant note. The very thought of the existence of the one true God makes demons tremble. The apostle James wrote: "Thou believest that there is one God; thou doest well: the devils also believe, and tremble" (2:19).

James indicated that the very fact there is a true, living, all-powerful God on His throne ruling in omnipotent majesty—that fact, and that alone, is enough to make demons tremble. If vile, fallen demons believe this and tremble, how much more should we humble ourselves before God and honor Him. No wonder David cried, "Let God arise, let his enemies be scattered" (Psalm 68:1).

The blood of Christ defeats demons on every battlefront. The writer of Hebrews said, "But this man, after he had offered one sacrifice for sins for ever, sat down on the right hand of God; from henceforth expecting till his enemies be made his footstool" (10:12, 13).

The blood of Christ cleanses us from all unrighteousness and has power over unrighteous beings. Demons cried out to Jesus, "What have we to do with thee, thou Jesus of Nazareth? art thou come to destroy us? I know thee who thou art, the Holy One of God" (Mark 1:24). Peter, Paul, and other giants of the New Testament era commanded demons to leave tortured souls "in the name of Jesus" (Acts 16:18).

Demons are real and they do have power, although it is limited. More of them probably are present and active in modern society than we can imagine. They are subtly working within many modern churches, attempting to dilute the gospel message, creating power cliques, and trying to make the church a strictly social organization. They are attacking families by slyly suggesting bringing things into the home that will eventually lead to moral decay and spiritual weakness. Probably there are more of these subtle, cunning demons at work than there are the obviously evil, monstrous type found in the Hollywood film world. It is time for the church to awake and shake itself in the power of the Holy Spirit. We must cry like David the shepherd did concerning the threat of Goliath of Gath: "Thy servant will go and fight" (1 Samuel 17:32).

We must whet our swords till the Word is keen as a razor and ready at our every need. We must fast to get ready to fight. We must pray the demons out from among us. Jesus identified particularly stubborn spirits like we face today and declared: "This kind goeth not out but by prayer and fasting" (Matthew 17:21).

CHAPTER 6

ANGELS: GOD'S MESSENGER WARRIORS

"The angel of the Lord encampeth round about them that fear him, and delivereth them" (Psalm 34:7).

Angels have always fascinated the imagination of mankind. As a result there has been much that is simply not true reported about angels. The literary world, with everything from the classics to modern science fiction, has added to the enormous amount of information human beings assume is true concerning angels. Angels have been portrayed as cuddly cupid-type creatures or secretive long-dead human beings on goodwill missions. Then, of course, there are angels in the Hollywood mold, like Clarence the 200-year-old clockmaker in *It's a Wonderful Life*, who earns his wings by returning to earth to save a suicide-bent businessman.

According to an article in *Time*, 69 percent of Americans believe in the existence of angels. *Time* reporter Nancy Gibbs relates that there are varied

75

opinions about the nature and composition of angels and that they are a part of the nomenclature of many religions.[1]

Since angels are very involved in spiritual warfare and the divine protection of the saints of God, it is imperative for us to understand the truth concerning them based on the real source of truth—the Word of God. Christ said, "Thy word is truth" (John 17:17).

Let us look first at what angels are not. A common belief is that when good people die they receive wings and harps and turn into angels. There is no biblical basis for this belief. It has been fostered by tradition and the ability of angels to move with great mobility, but there is no reference in Scripture where men who have died became angels. There are winged heavenly beings, such as the seraphim of Isaiah 6, and among the host of musical instruments in heaven there are harps (Revelation 14:2). In Revelation 5:8 we find 24 elders playing harps around the throne of God. These scriptural references were probably misconstrued centuries ago, and over the years a tradition developed of men becoming angels with wings and harps.

Actually, the redeemed will have a greater position of power and responsibility in eternity than the angels. The Bible says we will judge angels (1 Corinthians 6:3). The glorified redeemed will rule as kings and priests in the kingdom of God (Revelation 5:10). We will hold positions of enormous importance.

No, angels are not former men and women. They are not cuddly, cute Cupid-like figures. They are not mysterious and secretive beings who are on continual earthly missions.

The angels of God are created spiritual beings with many responsibilities, who live to serve and please God (Genesis 19:1; Psalm 34:7; 68:17; Mark 8:38; Hebrews

1:7). They are holy beings who reverence and fear God and do nothing contrary to His holy nature.

Angels praise and glorify God. Though we may not fully comprehend everything about their different spiritual forms, we do know all heavenly beings are submissive in their praise and adoration to God. The prophet Isaiah had a vision of God on His throne in the Temple, high and lifted up. Above God were angelic creatures, known as seraphim. "Each one had six wings; with twain he covered his face, and with twain he covered his feet, and with twain he did fly." They cried, "Holy, holy, holy, is the Lord of hosts: the whole earth is full of his glory" (Isaiah 6:32).

In Psalm 148:2, the angels were commanded to praise God, and in Daniel 7:10 we find "thousand thousands ministered unto him, and ten thousand times ten thousand" standing before the Ancient of Days ministering to Him in adoration.

Throughout the Book of Revelation, angels praise the worthiness of the Lamb that was slain. Special praise seems to be given in heaven to the Son of God for the great sacrifice He made to provide redemption and to defeat the devil, heaven's enemy.

Angels are messengers commissioned by God to bring messages to earth for men. The Bible cites many occasions when this occurred.

Three visitors came to Abraham on the plains of Mamre (Genesis 18). One of these visitors is identified as the Lord. Two of them went to Sodom to warn Lot of the impending doom on that city (v. 22). They are identified as angels in Genesis 19:1. They not only told Lot of the coming destruction, but they also had to smite with blindness the wicked men of Sodom who came to force themselves upon these visitors in an immoral fashion (v. 11). Lot's family had become so attached to Sodom and entangled in its web of evil that the angels had to evict Lot, his wife, and his two daughters from the city.

In Judges 6, while Israel was under siege by the hosts of Midian and a frightened farm boy named Gideon threshed his wheat in seclusion to hide it from foraging gangs of Midianites, an angel of the Lord appeared to him and said: "The Lord is with thee, thou mighty man of valour" (v. 12). Gideon asked the angel to show him a sign so he would know the Lord was with him. The angel asked for a present to be brought. Bread and meat was brought by Gideon and placed on a rock. The bread and meat was consumed by fire when the angel touched it with the staff he carried. Gideon feared he would die because he had seen an angel of the Lord face-to-face. The Lord told Gideon he would not die, but would have peace. Gideon became a great military leader and judge in Israel.

Gabriel is an angel often used as God's messenger. He brought messages to the prophet Daniel in Daniel 8 and 9. These messages from God concerning prophetic events and the nation of Israel will ultimately affect the entire world. Gabriel also appeared to Zacharias, the father of John the Baptist (Luke 1). Gabriel told the elderly priest that his elderly barren wife, Elizabeth, would conceive and give birth to a son (v. 13). Zacharias expressed doubt and asked for a sign. Gabriel answered, "I am Gabriel, that stand in the presence of God; and am sent to speak unto thee, and to shew thee these glad tidings" (v. 19). In other words, "How could I, who stands before God, speak anything but truth?" Then he said Zacharias would not be able to speak until all Gabriel told him had come to pass. Zacharias left the Temple unable to speak until John was born. Then his tongue was loosed and he "praised God" (v. 64).

ANGELS: GOD'S MESSENGER WARRIORS

Gabriel also brought the greatest news mankind has ever received. He appeared to Mary and told her she would be the mother of the Messiah (Luke 1:26-38).

Angels are described in the Bible as great warriors who can fight singly as individuals or band together as a mighty host.

Joshua 5 records that Joshua saw a man standing by Jericho with a drawn sword. He identified himself as "captain of the host of the Lord," and "Joshua fell on his face" (v. 14). The angel told Joshua, "Loose thy shoe from off thy foot; for the place whereon thou standest is holy" (v. 15). The next chapter tells how the seemingly impregnable city of Jericho fell, and all that God's people had to do was march and praise God. Surely an angelic host had fought the battle.

In 2 Kings 19, the Bible tells of the siege of Sennacherib of Assyria upon Jerusalem. This vain idol worshipper stopped the flow of water into the city and surrounded the city with a massive army and war machines. A godly king, Hezekiah, and a humble prophet, Isaiah, went into an inner chamber to pray while the pompous Sennacherib made fun of Jehovah and insulted the Hebrew nation. That night "the angel of the Lord went out" and smote 185,000 Assyrians. When Sennacherib arose the next morning, "they were all dead corpses" (v. 35). Sennacherib "returned with shame of face to his own land" (2 Chronicles 32:21), and two of his sons killed him when he went to worship his idol god, Nisroch, in Nineveh. In the final lines of Lord Byron's poem "The Destruction of Sennacherib," he gives a fitting epitaph for those who would war against God:

> And the might of the Gentile
> Unsmote by the sword
> Hath melted like snow
> In the glance of the Lord.

79

Often angels are placed in the role of rescuers. Elisha the prophet was rescued from Ben-hadad and the Syrian army by horses and chariots of fire that surrounded the enemy. On this occasion Elisha pronounced the immortal words: "Fear not: for they that be with us are more than they that be with them" (2 Kings 6:16).

An angel of the Lord warned Joseph in a dream to take Mary and the baby Jesus into Egypt to escape the death sentence of Herod, who ordered the slaying of all male children two years old and under living in Bethlehem and its vicinity (Matthew 2:13-16). An angel of God was sent into the innermost prison to rescue Peter on the eve of his intended execution by Herod (Acts 12). The angel did several miraculous things. The sleeping guards were in such a deep sleep they were not awakened when the chains fell from Peter's hands. The soldiers standing guard did not see Peter and the angel leave the prison. Locked doors and gates opened of their own accord.

Sometimes in the Bible angels did unique things. Jacob wrestled with an angel at Peniel and was never the same after that, for God blessed him (Genesis 32:24-30). The three Hebrew children shared a fiery furnace with an angel (Daniel 3). Balaam's donkey saw an angel before Balaam could see him (Numbers 22:25-35). The archangel Michael was sent to take the body of Moses and bury it. While performing this task, he was met by Satan, who wanted the body for his evil intent. The Bible says Michael didn't argue or make accusations against the devil but simply said, "The Lord rebuke thee" (Jude 9).

In the Book of Revelation angels of God blow trumpets of judgment (ch. 8), pour out God's wrath from vials upon the earth during the Tribulation period

ANGELS: GOD'S MESSENGER WARRIORS

(ch. 15), declare the end of time (10:5, 6), and announce the fall of apostate religion and Babylon (chs. 17, 18). A mighty angel comes down from heaven with a key to the bottomless pit and a chain in his hand, and he binds the devil and casts him into the pit for 1,000 years (20:1-3). One of the seven angels who poured out God's vials of wrath carried John to a high mountain to show him New Jerusalem descending (21:9, 10).

When Christ returns in midair to catch away the living and dead saints in the Rapture, a trumpet will sound, no doubt blown by an angelic musician. The Bible also says Christ will descend "with the voice of the archangel" (1 Thessalonians 4:16). Michael is the only angel referred to in the Bible as an archangel (Jude 9). In Daniel 12:1, Michael is called "the great prince." God told Daniel that at the time of the end, Michael will stand up for "the children of thy people . . . and at that time thy people shall be delivered, every one that shall be found written in the book." From these passages in Daniel and 1 Thessalonians we can deduct that at the sound of the trump of God and Christ's descent, Michael will utter his voice. Since Michael is seen biblically as a warrior fighting Satan (Daniel 10:13; Jude 9; Revelation 12:7-9), it is possible that his voice is the clarion call announcing the beginning of the end for the devil and all his forces as the bride joins Christ in the air, freed at last from their earthly pilgrimage.

Many times in Scripture angels present a frightening picture to mortal men. Their appearance was not necessarily intended to frighten. But God's purpose, rather, seems to have been to make them aware of His sovereignty and that higher powers are always present.

When God sent an angel to bring judgment on Israel because of David's sin of numbering the people, David saw an angel at the threshing floor of Ornan the

81

Jebusite. The angel was so massive, standing there with a drawn sword stretched over Jerusalem, that David must have trembled violently, for the Bible said he and the elders of Israel clothed themselves in sackcloth and fell upon their faces. This angel with the drawn sword, who had already slain 70,000 men, stood with his feet on the threshing floor and his head in the heavens. When David humbled himself, repented, sacrificed, and prayed, God commanded the angel, and he "put up his sword again into the sheath thereof" (1 Chronicles 21:27).

God's angels are real and powerful agents who serve God as messengers, warriors, or executioners of His wrath. They are characterized by obedience and perfection in the execution of their commanded duties.

We should note here that angels are sent to protect God's children and often fight spiritual battles for them. The great promise in Psalm 34:7—"The angel of the Lord encampeth round about them that fear him, and delivereth them"— has been a source of hope and comfort to God's people down through the centuries.

God's special agents known as angels visit people today. In their excellent work *War Beyond the Stars*, Joel and Jane French relate many stories of angelic encounters in modern times.[2] One such story concerns a missionary, Bill Loveck, who during his many years in Africa felt led to minister to a tribe of cannibals who had never been visited by a Christian missionary. When he shared his impression with the young African Bible student who was his guide, the young man became very upset. That particular tribe was notorious for eating the flesh of the young man's tribe.

Finally Loveck persuaded the young man that God was with them and would send His angels to protect

ANGELS: GOD'S MESSENGER WARRIORS

them. They traveled by jeep for several days into the African bush. Occasionally at night they would hear the roar of lions and other wild beasts. The young African stirred uneasily, but Loveck assured him God's angels would protect them.

Once, just before reaching their destination, they heard many voices and the rustling of bushes during the night. The next morning they discovered a circle of spears and knives around their jeep as if would-be attackers had left in a hurry.

After reaching the village the next day and telling the simple gospel message of Jesus Christ, they witnessed the salvation of nearly the whole tribe, including the chief. Among those who were saved was a group of young warriors who had intended to attack the jeep the night before. Immediately after accepting Christ, they excitedly asked the whereabouts of the two giant men with glowing white robes and long gleaming swords who had stood on either side of the jeep during the night. The two men in white apparel had suddenly appeared when the warriors approached the jeep. Frightened almost out of their wits, they dropped their weapons and ran from these supernatural beings.

I remember well a story from my childhood that has remained dear to my family for many years. This story brings to life the Scripture verse that says, "Be not forgetful to entertain strangers: for thereby some have entertained angels unawares" (Hebrews 13:2).

Many years ago my father was pastor of a church in a small Southern town. Though he had worked hard and labored untiringly on the church property, things seemed at a standstill spiritually. This was the mid-'50s and economic conditions were not the best. There were four of us small children in the family, and that year it seemed every childhood disease from whooping cough

83

SPIRIT WARS

to red measles was on the rampage. Mom was physically weak and in need of surgery; Dad was working around the clock to build and pastor his church; and we kids, like small stairsteps, were constantly needing attention.

****

He came on a Sunday morning early, around 8 o'clock. I still remember the intensely bright sunshine of that day, though I was only six at the time. He knocked on the door and I got there about the same time as Dad, who was wearing an apron over his Sunday suit. Dad was cooking breakfast while Mom tried to get us all ready for Sunday school. The man at the door looked like a hobo. He wore ragged clothes, an old faded gray suit, and a fedora that was sweat-stained and bent out of shape. His face was very red and ruddy and covered with a stubble of beard. I'll never forget his eyes—they danced and twinkled and were as blue as the noonday sky. He took off his hat and asked for something to eat. My dad invited him in and, to our astonishment, treated him like a dignitary of the highest importance. Dad fixed him breakfast, and as he put the plate in front of him, we all stared as only children will. The old man then bowed his head and my dad offered thanks. Dad invited him to church, and the old gentleman said he would be delighted.

That morning something very special happened. The choir sang as they had never sung. My dad preached under an anointing that was as if he were an ambassador from another world. The church was full that day, and many sinners were there. One by one they came to the altar and were wonderfully converted. The rejoicing of the saints and the tears of the redeemed were so overwhelming it made an impression on me as a child that I'll never forget. I'll never forget this either.

ANGELS: GOD'S MESSENGER WARRIORS

In the midst of the service I looked back to where our ragged visitor was sitting. Did God allow only me to see what I saw, or did everyone who looked see it also? I'll never know, but I do know I saw his face aglow with the glory of God. Big tears were rolling down his cheeks. I stood by Dad at the back door as people full of joy filed out of church that morning. Our friend stopped and shook Dad's hand, and mine, and grinned at me with that twinkle in his eye. I grinned back, my front teeth missing like all first graders. After he had departed—it hadn't been but a moment—Dad said, "David, run and ask the visitor if he wants to eat lunch with us." I ran down the tall front church steps and looked in the churchyard. He wasn't there. I looked down each street. Our church was on a corner and the land lay flat. You could see a long way down each street. There was no sign of the old gentleman. I ran to the back of the church. He was nowhere to be found, yet it had been but a moment. I came back and told Dad and Mom and they went outside and looked. We got in the car and drove through the streets trying to find him. Nothing! We believe we now know just how special our Sunday visitor was.

The church's time on this earth is growing shorter, and the fulfillment of biblical prophecy is a constant occurrence. The wars of the spirit world are increasing in intensity. We need to grasp the truth of Psalm 34:7, and we need to remember what God told Israel in Exodus 23:20: "Behold, I send an Angel before thee, to keep thee in the way, and to bring thee into the place which I have prepared."

"Are they not all ministering spirits, sent forth to minister for them who shall be heirs of salvation?" (Hebrews 1:14).

SPIRIT WARS

Endnotes

[1]Nancy Gibbs, "Angels," *Time*, Dec. 27, 1993, p. 27.

[2]Joel and Jane French, *War Beyond the Stars* (Harrison, Ark.: New Leaf Press, 1984), pp. 95, 96.

CHAPTER 7

THE WEAPONS OF OUR WARFARE

In the King James Version of the Bible, 2 Corinthians 10:3-5 reads: "For though we walk in the flesh, we do not war after the flesh: (For the weapons of our warfare are not carnal, but mighty through God to the pulling down of strong holds;) Casting down imaginations, and every high thing that exalteth itself against the knowledge of God, and bringing into captivity every thought to the obedience of Christ."

Now read the graphic translation of this powerful passage in *The New English Bible:* "Weak men we may be, but it is not as such that we fight our battles. The weapons we wield are not merely human, but divinely potent to demolish strongholds; we demolish sophistries and all that rears its proud head against the knowledge of God; we compel every human thought to surrender in obedience to Christ."

SPIRIT WARS

Tough talk? You had better believe it! The man who penned these words, under the divine inspiration of the Holy Spirit, was a hardened and scarred soldier of many battlefields of the spirit. Demons knew him by name and readily acknowledged they knew him and his best friend, Jesus of Nazareth (Acts 19:15).

Paul's back had been beaten so many times it must have looked like a basket weaver had intertwined his scars. He had known cold from lack of clothing, hunger from lack of food, loneliness from desertion of friends, and the violence of mobs directed solely toward him. He had clung to pieces of a broken sailing vessel for a day and a night as he precariously drifted toward an uncertain shore. He had hung in Roman stocks, smelled the stench of the sewer, and heard the sound of his blood dripping to the stone floor of a darkened dungeon (see 2 Corinthians 11:24-27). These things happened because of one simple fact: Paul was a preacher of the gospel, a soldier of the Cross, an ambassador of Christ Jesus, and a proclaimer of hope in a world without hope.

He talked tough because he had been toughened. He knew the war was not against flesh and blood. He told the Ephesians the Christian's warfare is a spirit war (Ephesians 6:12). Paul knew that and mastered his weaponry.

Paul boasted in the Lord, "We are more than conquerors" (Romans 8:37). And he declared, "I can do all things through Christ who strengthens me" (Philippians 4:13, *NKJV*). How could this giant of the New Testament world say these things? Simply put, Paul knew what was really going on in the flesh and in the spirit. He had come to the very true conclusion that the flesh, and everything that can be seen or that is material, is only temporary and the things which are

THE WEAPONS OF OUR WARFARE

not seen are eternal (2 Corinthians 4:18). Having understood this, he then knew the real war the saints must fight in this world is spiritual.

It then becomes easy to conclude it takes spiritual weapons to fight a spiritual war. Swords, spears, bows, and battering rams may be adequate in a war of the flesh; but in a war of the spirit, when the foe is formidable, greater weapons must be found. Hence, the declaration to the Corinthian church, "[Our] weapons . . . are not merely human, but divinely potent" (2 Corinthians 10:4).

Let us look at the arsenal of weaponry God has given to the body of Christ. We not only should be aware of their existence, but we should become skilled in their use. In Ephesians 6:13-19, Paul describes the armor a Christian should "put on." Much of our weaponry is described in these verses.

First, Paul said, "Take unto you the whole armour of God" (v. 13). Take the armor and prepare yourself, Paul was saying. Here, the picture is of a first-century Roman soldier. When he picks up his armor, the call to combat has been received and the battle is eminent.

After taking the armor, we are to put it on. Paul said we are to be "girt about with truth" (v. 14). The girdle, or belt (Greek, *zone*) was used to brace the armor tight against the body and support daggers, swords, and other weapons. Paul said *truth* is the belt that holds our weaponry together. Jesus said: "I am the way, the truth, and the life" (John 14:6); "Every one that is of the truth heareth my voice" (18:37); "Ye shall know the truth, and the truth shall make you free" (8:32); and, in a prayer to the Father as He prayed for His disciples, "Sanctify them through thy truth: thy word is truth" (17:17).

In other words, the truth of the Word of God holds

our armament together. Spiritual warfare is not a fantasy game drummed up by mystics with "a revelation" here and "a word" there as they develop rules and roles to combat territorial demons with bizarre names right out of the *Twilight Zone*. No, spiritual warfare is a war waged by the devil against the body of Christ and the truth of the gospel. And it is this great truth of the gospel that has set us free from our sin and enabled us to be victorious in these battles.

Next, Paul mentioned the "breastplate of righteousness" (v. 14). The Greek word used here is *thorax*, which was a breastplate in two parts to cover the upper chest and the vital organs, protecting the flow and circulation of life and covering the heart. Though our warfare is spiritual, we must live righteously and holy to protect the temple of God, our body, from the contamination of sin. Warriors who are riddled with sin-sickness are totally ineffective.

Paul then said our feet must be shod properly. This is in reference to the brazen boot which protected the front of the leg and had thick pads, or *soleas*, on the bottom to protect the feet from sharp objects and rocks. Paul says our footwear must be "the preparation of the gospel of peace" (Ephesians 6:15). Our feet should walk where the Prince of Peace leads us. Isaiah said, "Thou wilt keep him in perfect peace, whose mind is stayed on thee" (26:3). Our feet must "walk in the light, as he is in the light" (1 John 1:7). Feet led by the gospel of peace will not walk in darkness, for they follow the glow of the "light of the world" (John 8:12). Well-shod warriors' feet are steady and stable and provide a firm foundation in the heat of battle. They do not retreat while standing on Christ Jesus, the Rock, for they have never been—nor will they ever be—defeated by the greatest of hell's legions (Matthew 16:18).

THE WEAPONS OF OUR WARFARE

The "shield of faith" (v. 16) is translated from the Greek word *thureos*, which was a protector against blows and cuts. Our faith is "the substance of things hoped for, the evidence of things not seen," according to Hebrews 11:1. And by it we obtain "a good report" (v. 2).

The chapter continues with the mighty exploits of God's children, which, through the centuries, have been a result of faith. By faith Abel offered, Enoch was translated, Noah prepared, Abraham went out, Sarah received strength, Isaac and Jacob blessed, Joseph gave commandment, Moses refused and forsook Egypt, Jericho fell, Rahab perished not, kingdoms were subdued, righteousness was wrought, promises were obtained, lions' mouths were stopped, fire was quenched, swords were escaped, weakness was made strong, and alien armies turned to flight. Faith is the supershield. Satan's fiery darts bounce off it. We believe God and are protected.

The "helmet of salvation" (v. 17) protects the mind. Here the devil attacks first. Here he plants thoughts, arouses anger, cooks up revenge, and stirs our emotions. Here he would sow doubt and transplant roots of bitterness. We are redeemed, however. Our mind is now the mind of Christ. We pray for our enemies. We do good to those who despitefully use us. We render good for evil. If they want our coat, we give our cloak also. We know in our saved mind that a soft answer turns away wrath. We rejoice when persecuted, for great is our reward in heaven. In short, we wear the helmet of salvation. A redeemed mind makes us put away evil thinking.

Our weaponry is now enhanced by the offensive weapon we wield—"the sword of the Spirit, which is the word of God" (v. 17). How skillful we become with

SPIRIT WARS

this weapon depends on us. Our Bible, the sword of the Spirit, is "sharper than any twoedged sword . . . and is a discerner of the thoughts and intents of the heart" (Hebrews 4:12). It is so sharp in its poignant truth that it lays open the soul to reveal the real intent of the heart. The Word never returns to God void, but does what He sends it to do (Isaiah 55:11). In Christ's battle with Satan in the wilderness of temptation, Christ simply quoted God's Word from Deuteronomy and the result was "the devil left Him, and behold, angels came and ministered to Him" (Matthew 4:11, *NKJV*).

Paul then mentioned "prayer . . . watching . . . perseverance . . . supplication . . . utterance" (vv. 18, 19). These are tactics used in laying siege and must be dealt with if we are to be effective. Powerful weapons they are, and we need them to "pull down strongholds and bring things into captivity."

Prayer as a weapon is used here in the active sense. Paul was not talking about a formal prayer or part of a ceremonial exercise but of constant communication with God by the believer.

To gain a higher understanding of prayer in the life of the spiritual warrior, let us take the life of Christ as the supreme example. Though He was the only begotten Son of God, He lived on this earth in the robes of flesh. All man and yet all God, a combination hard to understand, He was God's gift to the world. And Jesus prayed. He had a constant, consistent prayer life. He stayed in close communication with the Father. So effective was His prayer life that the disciples—who were spiritually naive at first—soon began to associate His power and results of ministry with His prayer life. Their cry became, "Lord, teach us to pray" (Luke 11:1).

Christ's praying was from the heart. His prayers were not the loud utterances of ecclesiastical phraseology,

92

nor were they memorized poetry recited to impress listeners. His prayers came from the depths of His being, and the praises and requests were rooted in sincerity and need.

His prayer for the sanctification and divine keeping of His disciples (John 17) was a prayer that outmaneuvered any plans the devil might have had for their demise. Surely the devil would have liked to render the disciples ineffective as he scattered them in fear after Christ's death, but Jesus had prayed earnestly for them. He asked the Father to keep them from the evils of the world and to sanctify them through the Word. He reminded the Father that the world hated His disciples because the world hated Him. He also declared His plans to send them into the world even as He had been sent into the world, and He asked that while there they might have unity like that of the Father and Jesus.

What a prayer! Jesus prayed for everything His disciples, including all who would believe in the future, would need for victorious spiritual warfare. He prayed for holiness, unity, oneness with the Godhead, divine protection, glory, power, lives built on the Word, and boldness to go forward. The prayer of Jesus in John 17 is a model prayer of sincere open talk to the Father.

We should be praying—often, constantly, much, and in the greatest sincerity.

Several years ago, when my children were very small, in a time of family devotion we took turns praying. One of my children prayed in barely audible, whispering tones. At the close of the prayer, since the rest of the family had prayed aloud, I said to the child, "I couldn't hear you praying." The reply was classic and full of great spiritual truth: "Daddy, I wasn't praying to you." Though spoken with childish sweetness, the rebuke was powerful and effective. How true it is!

SPIRIT WARS

We are to pray to God and not to anyone else. The psalmist said, "This poor man cried, and the Lord heard him, and saved him out of all his troubles" (Psalm 34:6).

Watching is another great weapon Paul said is effective in the throes of the battle. Here we see the idea of alertness and keen observation. The Christian cannot be slack in spiritual alertness. God is not calling us to paranoia or a fear of evil, but He is warning us to be on the lookout. It is a very foolish soldier who doesn't watch for the ever-present reality of the enemy's possible attack.

We should not only watch for attacks by the enemy of our souls, but we should also watch for offensive opportunities. We should look for open doors of evangelism and gates of spiritual opportunity. There are times when God gives to us doors of effectual places and gaps in the Enemy's defenses where we can march forward for Christ and His cause on this earth. Often, God's people have missed possibilities for growth because no one was spiritually alert enough to seize the opportunity.

We also should watch our lives. It's good to examine ourselves. The best mirror available is the Word of God. The Bible commands this of believers: "Let a man examine himself" (1 Corinthians 11:28). Here Paul was talking about what a Christian should do before partaking of Communion. Paul said the heart and life should be searched during this sacred time of discerning the Lord's body. In 2 Corinthians 13:5 Paul said, "Examine yourselves, whether ye be in the faith; prove your own selves." Watchful soldiers will examine themselves, and if there are areas that make them unfit for battle, they will, with God's grace and power, cleanse themselves and gain strength in the process.

Perseverance is another weapon of effective power for

THE WEAPONS OF OUR WARFARE

the church. Here we are speaking of persistence. We cannot afford to give up. Quitting is not part of our vocabulary. The church of the Lord Jesus must never forget the words found in the message of Christ as He talked of end-time prophecy. In that powerful warning given in Matthew 24, the words of verse 13 stand out like a flashing beacon in the night: "But he that shall endure unto the end, the same shall be saved."

Paul then mentioned *supplication.* Supplication is petitioning, going after a certain thing with persistence. Jesus told the story of a judge who neither feared God nor regarded man (Luke 18:1-8). This judge, however, was petitioned constantly by a woman for justice in her particular case. The unjust judge finally granted her petition "lest by her continual coming she weary me" (v. 5). Jesus then drew this conclusion: "And shall not God avenge his own elect, which cry day and night unto him, though he bear long with them? I tell you that he will avenge them speedily" (vv. 7, 8).

Why have we overlooked this great spiritual principle? The early church knew the power of supplication. They petitioned God until Peter was set free from prison (Acts 12). They petitioned God until Paul and Barnabas were chosen to do missionary work (Acts 13). Cornelius petitioned God until God sent Peter with the gospel and power to his Gentile home (Acts 10). And the list could go on and on concerning the power of supplication.

The final thing Paul mentioned to the Ephesians in relationship to weaponry was *utterance.* So vital is this in our warfare that it is the subject of the next chapter.

My prayer, in writing about this next area of spiritual warfare, is the same as the apostle Paul's—"that therein I may speak boldly, as I ought to speak" (Ephesians 6:20).

CHAPTER 8

UTTERANCE THROUGH PREACHING: GOD'S CHOSEN WEAPON

"For after that in the wisdom of God the world by wisdom knew not God, it pleased God by the foolishness of preaching to save them that believe. For the Jews require a sign, and the Greeks seek after wisdom: but we preach Christ crucified, unto the Jews a stumblingblock, and unto the Greeks foolishness; but unto them which are called, both Jews and Greeks, Christ the power of God, and the wisdom of God" (1 Corinthians 1:21-24).

God has proven Himself to be a decisive and sovereign God. He has established rules, laws, and principles that both guide and guard the events of the universe. He has declared Himself to be unchangeable: "For I am the Lord, I change not" (Malachi 3:6). The psalmist declared in Psalm 115:3, "Our God is in the heavens: he hath done whatsoever he hath pleased."

God decided in His divine wisdom He would use the "foolishness of preaching" to save the world. In his first letter to the Corinthians, Paul explained why God chose this method. God wanted to use simple or base things to confound the wise, for even the foolishness of God is wiser than the wisdom of men. Paul reminded the Corinthians, some of whom evidently were called into the ministry, that God didn't necessarily call wise or mighty or noble men to preach the gospel, but rather He called simple vessels. Then when these vessels were anointed and used mightily to proclaim the powerful and productive gospel, no flesh would glory (1:26-29). Paul said, in verses 30, 31, that any wisdom, or righteousness, or sanctification (holiness), or redemption that we have as vessels comes from the Lord, and only in Him should we glory.

For centuries the church of the Lord Jesus Christ experienced the gleaning of the harvest and the molding of the body of Christ through the preaching of the Word. History is filled with examples of men who allowed themselves to be instruments called preachers. No one questioned the method. God had plainly said this was His method. Certainly other talents and gifts operated in the church, and God used a host of multitalented and gifted people; but for centuries it was understood that God's chief chosen method to convict men and women of sin and to spread the truth of Jesus Christ was preaching.

From the New Testament to modern times, we have seen those who, in spite of other abilities, were known most of all as preachers. The gallery is exciting to look at. Simon Peter, Apollos, the apostle Paul, John the son of Zebedee, Clement, Augustine, Martin Luther, John Knox, John Huss, George Whitfield, John Wesley, David Brainerd, Charles G. Finney, Charles Spurgeon, Dwight L. Moody, Sam Jones, Billy Sunday, R.P. Johnson, Billy Graham, and Ray H. Hughes are but a few of the pulpit giants who have stirred the hearts of listeners with the preached gospel of Christ. But joining these are a vast host of less known, but equally called, men and women who have willingly given themselves as vessels of honor to preach the gospel. And God has honored their willingness by anointing them to proclaim the Word of Life.

Now something very dangerous is happening in the world of Christendom as we near the end of the 20th century. Few people are recognizing it or realizing what the terrible consequences will be, but Satan is deliberately seeking to downplay the importance of the preaching of the Word. He has succeeded in developing elements in the body that no longer see its importance and seek to relegate preaching to a secondary role. Their cry and belief is that we must modernize the approach of evangelism and discipleship to conform to the times. Programs that present the gospel in the form of entertainment, sharing groups, Bible-search cells, drama, videos, and computerized self-help discipleship courses are promoted as the wave of the future. The same segment of Christian society says everyone is a preacher. They also say that in a corporate service the proclamation should be soft and spoken naturally, with anyone who feels an impression free to give a word or revelation of truth. There also is an alarming tendency among these advocates of radical change to demean traditional preaching—especially the way a preacher's voice changes as he begins his delivery and the strenuous demonstrative preaching of many Evangelicals and Pentecostals.

Let's sift through the confusion and try to get a biblical perspective.

God has placed many gifts in the church. The Bible says God placed them as He willed (1 Corinthians

12:11). Certainly diversity beautifies the body of Christ. I never cease to be amazed at how God distributes the work load of the church among so many unique and diverse groups of people.

And let me say emphatically God can use a multiplicity of programs, a menagerie of electronic and computerized equipment, creative study groups of every nature, and masterfully written plays and songs of all sorts. After all, if God used a storm, a whale, a gourd vine, and a worm to teach the prophet Jonah several object lessons about mercy, forgiveness, and the importance of lost souls, He can use 20th-century gadgetry for His purposes. He who made the sun to stand still in Joshua's day to defeat the Amorites can use a video machine to mesmerize a group of 4-year-olds and make them sit still long enough to learn about God's love.

The danger is not in programs or enhancement methods to train and equip the church. The danger lies in a cynicism that is developing toward preachers and the preaching of the gospel. What has brought this on? I believe this attitude is a wound that has been received in last-day spiritual warfare. What caused this grievous wound?

First, we have witnessed something most unusual— the public downfall and humiliation of popular clergymen due to immorality. The media has had a heyday with this. Unfortunately, society often lumps all members of the same profession together. Like other maligned professionals, the clergy has become the object of public scrutiny and ridicule.

Second, this is a fulfillment of biblical prophecy. Because false prophets have arisen in the last days, like the Bible said they would, and because many are making merchandise of the gospel, like the Bible said they would, a crisis of confidence has arisen concerning the

UTTERANCE THROUGH PREACHING: GOD'S CHOSEN WEAPON

ministry. Since many people no longer have confidence in the messengers, they disregard all messages. This is great error on their part and dangerous for the welfare of their soul.

In 1 Kings 19, Elijah the prophet made a serious error in judgment. He believed he was the only one who was faithfully serving God and proclaiming the truth. God rebuked him sternly and told him He had 7,000 in Israel who had never bowed a knee to Baal (v. 18). God also told Elijah he was not indispensable and that He had someone to take Elijah's place when he was gone and good kings waiting in line to replace evil Ahab.

The lesson is plain. Though some may fall to error and sin, there are many faithful servants of the Lord who preach the truth Sunday after Sunday. And because God has called them and given them the task of preaching the message of life, we should listen to what they say.

God takes it as a personal affront when His prophets and preachers are despised. God said, "Touch not mine anointed, and do my prophets no harm" (1 Chronicles 16:22; Psalm 105:15). God will judge and deal with a backslidden preacher living in sin, but the same God will defend very jealously a humble man who, in the fear of the Lord, has given his life to preach the gospel.

Another reason preaching is being despised in the last days is that people do not want to be reproved and convicted of wrong. The tragedy is that society does not want to hear what is wrong and right. Like ancient Israel in the days of Samuel, every man wants to do what is right in his own eyes. Paul told Timothy that in the last days people would look for teachers who would say and teach things that pleased their ears (2 Timothy 4:3).

Since most of the free world is blessed with a multiplicity of churches, people who are offended at the truth simply go somewhere else or, if enough are offended, they make the preacher go somewhere else. This problem of refusing to accept the truth must be corrected.

An enormous responsibility falls upon the God-called preacher if he is to be an instrument of God and rightly divide the Word of truth: he must seek God for his messages. If his pulpit crutch is "Randy's Really Rousing Ready-to-Read Sermon Nuggets" and he is shortchanging the precious flock of God due to spiritual laziness, he will face an awesome God in judgment and the blood of souls who might have been won will be on his hands (Ezekiel 33:6-8).

According to the Bible itself, the Word is "quick, and powerful, and sharper than any twoedged sword, piercing even to the dividing asunder of soul and spirit, and of the joints and marrow, and is a discerner of the thoughts and intents of the heart" (Hebrews 4:12). What a weapon! To wield it, one must study to show himself approved to God, a workman that doesn't have to be ashamed or embarrassed (2 Timothy 2:15).

This hour desperately needs the anointed preaching of the Word by consecrated vessels. Preaching the whole counsel of God will bring revival to an apostate church and bring conviction upon the unsaved listeners. Faith has to come by hearing, and hearing must come by the Word of God (Romans 10:17).

A minister of my acquaintance tells of a time he was visited by a certain parishioner. This individual had been attending the minister's church for several months when he scheduled the appointment and made the visit to the minister's office. The person began to ask in all sincerity if the minister was involved with any law enforcement agency or was a private investigator of any sort. The person was very nervous and explained to the

UTTERANCE THROUGH PREACHING: GOD'S CHOSEN WEAPON

pastor that because of his preaching of the Word about sins of dishonesty and unethical behavior, he had come under conviction for wrongs he had committed. He sincerely thought the clergyman might be privy to some secret information about his sins. When the pastor explained to him that his only source of information was the Bible and what it says about sin, the realization that God was watching gripped the man's heart and he repented and experienced a transformation. There is enormous power in anointed preaching.

We who are called to proclaim the truth must live by the truth we proclaim. We must guard our lives and not place ourselves in compromising positions by giving place to the devil. Though we are just as human as any other Christian, and no holier nor more redeemed than anyone else, we do have the highest calling God can give in Christian service. Charles Spurgeon once said, "If a man is a God-called preacher, why should he stoop to be a king?"

In spite of the disdain toward the preaching ministry, no preacher of the gospel should bow his head in shame of his profession. He, like the angels in the shepherds' field on the first Christmas night, is proclaiming good tidings of great joy! We are ambassadors of the Prince of Peace! Isaiah declared, "How beautiful upon the mountains are the feet of him that bringeth good tidings, that publisheth peace; that bringeth good tidings of good, that publisheth salvation; that saith unto Zion, Thy God reigneth!" (52:7). No wonder the devil wants to make disparaging remarks about preachers of the gospel. No wonder we who are called to preach must conduct ourselves in such a way as to "let not . . . [our] good be evil spoken of" (Romans 14:16). We have a sacred trust and a commissioned task.

Preaching can be a weapon of great importance in

103

spiritual warfare. Anointed preaching is instructional to the believer, comforting to the downtrodden, encouraging to those in despair, inspiring to those who need leadership, and convicting to those guilty of sin. It can also shake the foundations of hell and send a trembling through demonic ranks. When Jesus preached, demons cried out in protest saying, "What have we to do with thee, thou Jesus of Nazareth?" (Mark 1:24). Powerful preaching has always made the devil nervous, and the reason is simple: the sword of the Spirit is cutting and tearing down the trouble he has built in human lives.

The greatest failure the church could ever suffer would be to stop preaching the gospel. There are those who try to minimize preaching with phrases like "It's not that important in overall ministry" or "You have to do more than just be able to preach!" While it is true that a preacher often has a diversity of responsibilities and tasks to perform, these verbal attacks on preaching are not just statements of work definition. Those who make such statements are making a deliberate attempt to minimize the importance of the preached Word of God. They should examine themselves and ask God to forgive them for minimizing the method He chose to save the world.

When the translators of the King James Version of the Bible wrote their famous preface and addressed it to King James, they made a statement that is noteworthy for us today: "But among all our joys, there was no one that more filled our hearts, than the blessed continuance of the preaching of God's sacred Word among us; which is that inestimable treasure, which excelleth all the riches of the earth; because the fruit thereof extendeth itself, not only to the time spent in this transitory world, but directeth and disposeth man unto that eternal happiness which is above in heaven."

UTTERANCE THROUGH PREACHING: GOD'S CHOSEN WEAPON

What a statement of beauty and purpose concerning the preaching of God's Word! These dedicated translators of the Scripture sincerely felt that for their age and time there was no treasure that could be given a nation more valuable than the continuance of the preaching of God's Word. They said this treasure was "inestimable."

The first thing a godless dictatorial power does when seizing control of a government is to stop the preaching of God's Word. Adolph Hitler did it in Nazi Germany. The Bolsheviks did it in Soviet Russia. Mussolini did it in fascist Italy. Mao Tse-tung and his henchmen did it in Communist China. And the list goes on. The reason is that the Bible teaches peace, joy, freedom, brotherhood, and the laws of justice and equality. Demon-inspired men want this stopped. This weapon is too much for them. The people's hearts are turned to good through anointed preaching, and their purposes of evil cannot be served.

A revival of anointed Bible preaching is needed in these last days. Abraham Lincoln said, "When I see a man preach, I like to see him preach as if he were fighting bees!" The great emancipator wanted his preaching seasoned with fiery fervor and godly zeal.

When Paul stood on trial, in one of a series of trials that would eventually lead to his martyrdom, he made a statement that should be every anointed preacher's statement of determination regardless of how the rest of the world feels. In his second letter to Timothy he told his young protege this stirring truth: "At my first answer no man stood with me, but all men forsook me: I pray God that it may not be laid to their charge. Notwithstanding the Lord stood with me, and strengthened me; that by me the preaching might be fully known, and that all the Gentiles might hear: and I was delivered out of the mouth of the lion. And the Lord

105

shall deliver me from every evil work, and will preserve me unto his heavenly kingdom: to whom be glory for ever and ever. Amen" (4:16-18).

CHAPTER 9

PULLING DOWN STRONGHOLDS AND BRINGING INTO CAPTIVITY

When a brilliant military general plans his strategy of conquest, he utilizes all he has learned to outwit and outmaneuver the enemy. He knows he must never bypass a strong enemy fortification and leave it unscathed. He cannot afford to leave enemy troops in the rear of his army, lest he be cut off and destroyed from both sides. Fortifications must be overcome if the campaign is to be successful. The enemy must not be allowed to remain strong and sheltered.

Satan and his fallen angels and demon hordes have shared this planet with the human race since Adam and Eve were driven from Eden's paradise. They have not been idle, but they continually build and fortify their protectorates and areas of dominion.

The Scripture is the truth of God and does not contradict itself, but we must, as we are commanded to, rightly divide the Word of Truth (2 Timothy 2:15). Thus we must reconcile two Bible passages. The Bible calls

Satan "the god of this world" (2 Corinthians 4:4). The Bible also says that "the earth is the Lord's, and the fulness thereof; the world, and they that dwell therein" (Psalm 24:1). Notice the distinction. The worldly system, which is unredeemed and apart from the true God, looks up to Satan, with his evil and greedy system, as a god or idol. But the true God of heaven is the real owner of the earth and everything and everybody in it. Satan, then, is here only by permission and is an interloper. Jesus labeled him as "the thief" who comes "to steal, and to kill, and to destroy" (John 10:10).

When we understand Psalm 24:1, we are made to realize that any strongholds or places of power Satan has built in this earth, be they physical or spiritual, have been built on territory he doesn't own. We are God's heirs of promise, God's children by adoption, and redeemed by the precious blood of Christ. Make no mistake about it, we are in a spiritual position to pull down satanic strongholds and bring thoughts into captivity until they desire only to obey Christ.

What is the scriptural truth about territorial spirits? Much false doctrine that borders on fantasy and sensationalism has been taught and written concerning spiritual warfare and territorial spirits. Though these teachings often come from sincere and well-meaning Christians, they are sometimes the product of overactive, zealous imaginations and the purported revelations of well-meaning people in scriptural error. No teaching that goes beyond the Word of God, either by adding to the Word or by taking away from the Word, will benefit the body of Christ. Confusion will ensue as a result of such teachings, and schisms will develop in the body that will cause long-lasting hurt. In many cities, misguided fanaticism concerning spiritual warfare and territorial spirits has caused people to have public "bindings and rebukings" of such spirits that

PULLING DOWN STRONGHOLDS AND BRINGING INTO CAPTIVITY

were nothing more than public exorcisms. In many of these cases, actual records show there was no decrease in sin, crime, immorality, or any other devil-inspired activity. Does this mean Satan cannot be dealt with corporately by the body of Christ? Absolutely not! But it does mean we must be totally biblical in order to get biblical results. New Testament methods reap New Testament results. Scriptural practices work.

I believe there is biblical evidence territorial spirits and satanic strongholds exist. In Daniel 10, Daniel the prophet was told by the angel Gabriel that when he first began his prayer, God sent Gabriel with an answer. But as Gabriel traveled with God's message, a demonic spirit labeled as the ruler of the geographic territory of Persia withstood or battled with him. The deadlock was broken, according to Gabriel in verse 13, when Michael the archangel came to help him. Even then, Gabriel said he stayed there for a time with other territorial rulers of Persia until he was free to come to Daniel. This passage tells us there are spirit wars in the spirit world.

In verse 9 of his short but powerful epistle, Jude relates the story of a battle for the body of Moses fought by Michael the archangel and Satan. Many Bible scholars believe God purposely hid forever the body of Moses, lest the Jews would enshrine him as an object of worship like Islam has done with the tomb of Muhammad. Perhaps Satan had this in mind. For what other reason would he want the body of Moses, a great Jewish leader? Michael's strategy was brilliant and powerful. He did not, like some would do, bring a "railing accusation" against Satan. He simply said, "The Lord rebuke thee."

Evil spirits rule over certain areas of emotion and the occult. There are spirits that foster fear, doubt, dissen-

109

SPIRIT WARS

sion, strife, anger, wrath, lust, revenge, and other emotions that war with our soul. The writer of Hebrews warns of the consequences of "an evil heart of unbelief" (3:12). Evil spirits also are behind the occult and the world of magic. Paul, in Acts 16, cast a demon of fortune-telling out of the damsel of Philippi.

Satan and his cohorts are here by permission. Not only is much of the human race still unredeemed, but none of the human race has yet been glorified. We still await "the redemption of our body" (Romans 8:23). The earth and creation are "subject to vanity" (v. 20), and the whole creation groans, waiting for the "manifestation of the sons of God" (v. 19).

We then will not totally eradicate Satan and his demon forces from this earth during the church age prior to the Rapture. What we must concentrate on is pulling down his strongholds, casting down vain imaginations, and bringing thoughts into obedience to Christ (2 Corinthians 10:4, 5).

Prayer is the great machine of power in spiritual warfare. The Bible says, "The eyes of the Lord are over the righteous, and his ears are open unto their prayers" (1 Peter 3:12). Jesus taught His disciples that "men ought always to pray, and not to faint" (Luke 18:1). Paul taught the church of Thessalonica to "pray without ceasing" (1 Thessalonians 5:17). When Peter was imprisoned by Herod and awaiting public execution, "prayer was made without ceasing of the church unto God for him" (Acts 12: 5). Did it work? It worked swiftly and miraculously. An angel arrived and set him free. The angel found Peter sleeping so soundly he "smote" him to awaken him. Imagine that! This man of God was sleeping soundly on the eve of his scheduled execution. Perhaps he knew the church was praying. So, why not sleep if your life is in God's care?

110

PULLING DOWN STRONGHOLDS AND BRINGING INTO CAPTIVITY

Look at some other biblical answers to prayer where circumstances existed due to satanic work.

Daniel's prayer life caused him to be singled out for execution in a den of lions. The same prayer life caused him to spend a harmless night among these hungry beasts (Daniel 6).

Israel was humiliated by the tiny village of Ai after the fall of mighty Jericho. This happened because Achan, a man of Israel, had taken things out of Jericho that God had cursed and were forbidden. Joshua, Israel's leader, fell prostrate and began to pray. God revealed the problem to Joshua; lots were cast and Achan was singled out from among hundreds of thousands of Israelites. Achan was destroyed, and Israel went forward (Joshua 7).

Ahab and Jezebel worshiped the demon gods, Baal and Ashtoreth, even though they were king and queen of Israel. During their heathen worship, they butchered children, put their severed body parts in stone pots, and buried them before satanic altars. They also performed lewd sex acts on high places before their idols. Elijah, God's prophet, prayed and a three-and-one-half-year famine followed. Elijah prayed on Mount Carmel, and God sent down fire and disgraced the prophets of Baal, who were on Jezebel's personal payroll. Elijah prayed again, and rain came to end the drought. A prophecy was given concerning the exact nature of Ahab and Jezebel's deaths, and it came to pass to the letter (1 Kings 16—18; 21; 2 Kings 9).

Jesus told Simon Peter on one occasion, "Satan hath desired to have you, that he may sift you as wheat: but I have prayed for thee, that thy faith fail not" (Luke 22:31, 32). Notice Satan's power and intent. Jesus said the devil could sift a man as wheat. When wheat is sifted, it is divided and separated, and part of it is blown

111

away and becomes useless. The rest is devoured, after it is crushed and baked in a hot oven. So Satan desired to divide, crush, and devour Simon Peter, but Jesus prayed for him.

In Acts 13, a powerful sorcerer named Elymas tried to hinder the ministry of Paul and Barnabas. These men of God, full of the Holy Spirit, faced the priest of Satan and slave of the occult, and Paul's prayer left Elymas blind and powerless, having to be led about like an invalid (vv. 8-11).

Prayer gets the attention of God. The prayers of the saints are stored in vials before the throne and continually make heaven fragrant with their sweet aroma (Revelation 5:8).

Several years ago, a pastor friend of mine was especially distressed, and so was his church. The church was in a rural location and was reached by one main highway from the small town where most of the congregation lived. On that same highway was a drive-in theater, facing the road, that showed pornographic movies. The people were embarrassed and offended with this blatant disregard for decency facing them on their way to church.

The church decided to band together one spring night for prayer regarding this matter. Petitions to the authorities had done no good, and the owner wouldn't be reasoned with. That night the church prayed in earnest for God to intervene and stop Satan's work. While they prayed, a thunderstorm arose in the county. Lightning struck the drive-in screen and burned it to the ground. Shall we call this coincidence? I think not! Again, heaven landed a powerful blow against a physical satanic stronghold.

Not only must we pray, but we need to also learn to agree on good things and needful things. The Scripture

PULLING DOWN STRONGHOLDS AND BRINGING INTO CAPTIVITY

is plain: "If two of you shall agree on earth as touching any thing that they shall ask, it shall be done for them of my Father which is in heaven" (Matthew 18:19). We have been so taken back by the "name it and claim it," "confess it and possess it" faith perversions of the 1980s that we have been afraid to get back to a powerful New Testament concept that has been successfully used throughout the history of Pentecost. We do not want to be warped in our concepts of faith. We do not agree for greed, gain, fame, power, or prestige. We use Matthew 18:19 as a premise to believe together scripturally for things within the framework of Scripture and the will of God. We should agree that if it is His will, what we are agreeing upon will happen. And it is His will that we overcome the world, defeat the devil, and be victorious in Christ Jesus.

We also must use the teaching of sound doctrine to pull down strongholds. Paul told Timothy that a phenomenon of the last days would be an increase of false teachers, teaching things that please people's ears (2 Timothy 4:3, 4). A sound doctrine is compatible with the entire Bible, from Genesis to Revelation. Real scriptural truth is not based on one scripture taken out of context. Sound doctrine will not cause confusion and do hurt to the body of Christ, for God is not the author of confusion (1 Corinthians 14:33). In fact, the Word of God will build us up and give us an inheritance (Acts 20:32). Over the centuries, the teaching of Christianity in its soundness has brought civilization and truth to lands ravaged by disease, cannibalism, idolatry, war, and savagery. The greatest cure rates for those who are alcohol and drug dependent are among Christian institutions where the addicts are not only set free from their addictions but are taught the Word of God and led into a relationship with Christ.

113

SPIRIT WARS

Is this spiritual warfare? Yes, of the highest sort. Here lives on the brink of destruction are released from the demonic grip.

Sound doctrine literally means doctrine that is firm, stable, and irrefutable. We live in a world plagued by instability. Leadership in government changes constantly, institutions fall, fashions change erratically, and society is colored by fads that come and go. Few things remain constant, but the Word of God never changes.

There are some basics in the portfolio of sound doctrine that when taught act as mighty battering rams against Satan's strongholds. They are irrefutable and nonnegotiable.

The first is the doctrine of Christ. He was born of a virgin (Isaiah 7:14; Matthew 1:18-25; Luke 1:26-38). This Virgin Birth fulfilled God's requirements for the Redeemer to be without sin (Genesis 3:15). He was God's only begotten Son (John 3:16; Hebrews 1:5, 6). He came to give His life a ransom for the souls of all men (Matthew 20:28). He died on the cross on a hill called Golgotha (John 19:17, 18, 30). He was raised from the dead and has become the firstfruits of the Resurrection (Matthew 28:6; 1 Corinthians 15:20). He has ascended back to the Father, where He ever lives to make intercession for us (Acts 1:9, 10; Hebrews 7:25). He will come again (John 14:3; Acts 1:11; 1 Thessalonians 4:16).

Another nonnegotiable doctrine is the inerrancy of the Scripture. We believe in the verbal inspiration of the Bible. Peter said it plainly: "Knowing this first, that no prophecy of the scripture is of any private interpretation. For the prophecy came not in old time by the will of man: but holy men of God spake as they were moved by the Holy Ghost" (2 Peter 1:20, 21). The Bible's testimony of itself is moving. Christ said, "Heaven and

114

PULLING DOWN STRONGHOLDS AND BRINGING INTO CAPTIVITY

earth shall pass away, but my words shall not pass away" (Matthew 24:35). Isaiah wrote, "The grass withereth, the flower fadeth: but the word of our God shall stand for ever" (40:8).

Perhaps one of our greatest doctrines that should be taught and believed is the doctrine of the sovereignty of God. God reigns supreme. We believe He is sovereign and doesn't change, lie, or make mistakes. He is just and altogether good and holy. I can't explain all His decisions, for I am finite and limited in my faculties. But I agree completely with the prophet Isaiah, who said to the cynics of his day who dared question God's authority and sovereignty: "Who hath measured the waters in the hollow of his hand, and meted out heaven with the span, and comprehended the dust of the earth in a measure, and weighed the mountains in scales, and the hills in a balance? Who hath directed the Spirit of the Lord, or being his counsellor hath taught him? With whom took he counsel, and who instructed him, and taught him in the path of judgment, and taught him knowledge, and shewed to him the way of understanding?" (40:12-14).

We teach sound doctrine to combat error and to plant gospel seed on fertile soil. We know that when men and women are birthed in Christ with teaching and preaching of sound doctrine, they are born into stability, for they are begotten of the Word.

Maybe territories and whole cities are not changed, but never in human history has 100 percent of the populace of this planet accepted the truth. Christ said some seed will fall on stony ground, or by the wayside, or among thorns; only a percentage will fall on fertile soil. But we reap where we can. We win men one at a time as individuals.

How do we win? It's really very simple: "For

115

SPIRIT WARS

whatsoever is born of God overcometh the world: and this is the victory that overcometh the world, even our faith. Who is he that overcometh the world, but he that believeth that Jesus is the Son of God?" (1 John 5:4, 5).

CHAPTER 10

STANDING: THE POWER OF WAITING

"And Moses said unto the people, Fear ye not, stand still, and see the salvation of the Lord, which he will shew to you to day: for the Egyptians whom ye have seen to day, ye shall see them again no more for ever. The Lord shall fight for you, and ye shall hold your peace" (Exodus 14:13, 14).

How often, in the heat of an intense spiritual struggle, have we pursued blindly ahead, offensively, as if the very act of forging ahead would win the battle for us? We become masters of spiritual tactics and do good things, yet often see no results. Maybe we need to stop, be still, and listen to the Lord. The power of waiting for God has almost become a lost treasure for the last-day church. We need to rediscover what a wonderful and powerful strategy it is to "stand still."

First, it often is commanded in Scripture. After many readings of God's commands to "stand," even stubborn Christian warriors who continually want to

SPIRIT WARS

rush ahead should realize God is trying to get a message through to His people.

In Exodus 14, Israel was on the shores of the Red Sea. Wilderness sand was beneath their sandals and a swift army of Pharaoh's elite troops was bearing down on them. Death seemed imminent to Israel. In this precarious situation Moses told Israel, "Stand still, and see the salvation of the Lord" (v. 13). He did not command them to search for anything that could be used for a weapon. He did not use his multitudes of able-bodied men as a wall of defense between the Egyptians and the women and children of Israel. He simply told them to wait and see God's deliverance: "The Lord shall fight for you, and ye shall hold your peace" (v. 14).

Well, that is it! The battle's over! God never loses! He has never lost, nor will He ever lose in the future. That day God divided the sea, made the water become walls, dried the soggy seafloor, allowed a nation safe passage across the seafloor, pulled the wheels off 600 Egyptian chariots, pulled down the water walls on the Egyptian army, and then enjoyed the praise celebration started by a 94-year-old Israelite tambourine player named Miriam. If God says, "Stand still," then "freeze."

Scripture is replete with such advice from God and His servants. God commanded the priests who carried the ark of the covenant to "stand still" in the flooded waters of Jordan (Joshua 3:8), and the miracle of the crossing occurred.

The prophet commanded young Saul to "stand still" so Samuel could show him the Word of God (1 Samuel 9:27). The Word still is best learned in quiet meditation—standing still and listening while God speaks.

Samuel told Israel, "Now therefore stand still, that I may reason with you before the Lord of all the right-

118

STANDING: THE POWER OF WAITING

eous acts of the Lord, which he did to you and to your fathers" (1 Samuel 12:7). Things could be explained and good sense could rule the day when God's people took time to listen to sound reason.

The patriarch Job, the great example of patience, was told to "stand still, and consider the wondrous works of God" (Job 37:14). At the time, Job was covered from the crown of his head to the soles of his feet with festering, ulcerating boils. He had become skin stretched over a skeleton. His children had died in a horrible disaster. He had gone from wealth to abject poverty. His wife advised him to curse God and die. His friends accused him of hidden sin and hypocrisy. He had lamented, "My breath is corrupt, my days are extinct, the graves are ready for me" (17:1). In the midst of this portrait of misery, Job was told to refocus his attention and to stand still and consider the wondrous works of God. So often, as we focus on ourselves and our circumstance, we feel overwhelmed in our spiritual battles. Here is the grand solution: "Consider the wondrous works of God." We have to be still to do this. Here is an overlooked tactic of spiritual warfare. Several grand things take place when we stand still and consider the works of God.

First, the very act of considering God's works means our minds are off our circumstances. Our situation may be fraught with danger, fear, satanic attack, discouragement, need, and physical infirmity. But when we take our eyes off what plagues us and look to the wondrous works of God, then we see His power at work all around us.

Second, a glimpse of His wondrous works builds our faith. Miracles can be seen everywhere in such works of God as the precise rotation of the earth, the unfailing power of gravity, the cycles of weather and seasons, the

119

longevity and triumph of the church, the preservation of the Bible, a tree rooted and living on stony ground, the tides of great oceans, and the rising of the sun. He is there and He is not silent, nor does He sleep or slumber. When we behold His works, our faith in Him soars and our circumstances shrink beside His never-failing omnipotence.

Third, beholding His wondrous works generates praise within us that soon becomes vocal. The good news is that things happen when we start to praise. God comes down among us, for He inhabits the praises of His people (Psalm 22:3). When God inhabits our praise, the loving, benevolent, and merciful ruler of heaven and earth is present, and with Him there is no impossibility. Our praise soon leads to prayer and petition. His eyes are upon the righteous, and His ears are open to our every prayer (Psalm 34:15).

Finally, when we behold His wondrous works while standing still, we are filled with resolve. Looking at a mountain teaches stability. Listening to a babbling brook brings peace. Smelling a gardenia teaches us that only God can create real beauty. Determination sets in and we are not so easily moved and tossed about by life's trials.

Not only do we need to learn to stand still, but we also must learn to wait for power. David, the man after God's own heart, said much about waiting. In Psalm 25:3, he said, "Yea, let none that wait on thee be ashamed." In verse 5, David declared, "On thee do I wait all the day." He talked of waiting power in Psalm 27:14: "Wait on the Lord: be of good courage, and he shall strengthen thine heart: wait, I say, on the Lord." In the face of his enemy's overwhelming strength, David said, "Because of his strength will I wait upon thee: for God is my defense" (59:9).

STANDING: THE POWER OF WAITING

Isaiah's passage about the power of waiting offers hope to today's stressed-out Christians: "Hast thou not known? hast thou not heard, that the everlasting God, the Lord, the Creator of the ends of the earth, fainteth not, neither is weary? there is no searching of his understanding. He giveth power to the faint; and to them that have no might he increaseth strength. Even the youths shall faint and be weary, and the young men shall utterly fall: but they that wait upon the Lord shall renew their strength; they shall mount up with wings as eagles; they shall run, and not be weary; and they shall walk, and not faint" (40:28-31).

What is the prophet saying to us? Everybody gets weary and tired and stressed and fainthearted—everyone except God. He doesn't succumb to fatigue and weariness of the spirit or body. Wait for Him. He'll bring you fresh water and nourishment. He will restore you from your weariness with a supernatural strength that will quicken you in the midst of the worst battle fatigue.

Before the outpouring of the Holy Spirit on the Day of Pentecost, the disciples were commanded to tarry in Jerusalem, waiting for this marvelous outpouring of power (Luke 24:49). They waited, the promise came, and the world has never been the same.

Waiting should be a time of prayer, praise, and supplication. Here is the time both to intercede and to listen for God's communication with you. If prayer is communication, why should we do all the talking?

Sometimes the greatest problems Christians find themselves in are those that occur when they move too hastily and attempt to solve problems in the power of the flesh. A phrase stands out in the Book of Acts concerning a decision the early church was about to make: "For it seemed good to the Holy Ghost, and to us"

(15:28). Here we find the Spirit of God and Christians in one accord on the same decision.

An old saying makes sense: "Haste makes waste." Why should we rush into decisions and operate on strategy devised by the flesh when we can wait for God, allowing Him to work and give us the power to move forward?

The church waited in fervent prayer until the place of their assembly was shaken, and they were all filled with the Holy Ghost and spoke the Word of God with boldness (Acts 4:31).

Paul and Silas waited in the dungeon of Philippi until an earthquake came and brought a revival. Peter waited on the rooftop of Simon's seaside home in Joppa until the vision of ministry to the Gentiles came. The Ethiopian eunuch waited in the desert until God sent Philip to explain Isaiah 53. John waited in the spirit on Patmos until he received the Revelation. We live in the society of the space shuttle, the microwave, the blow dryer, the remote control, the computer mouse, and presweetened Kool-Aid. We have forgotten some things are worth waiting for.

The foe we face is so formidable that we must wait for a higher power. Weary warrior, listen to these verses that offer hope and the best advice you can receive: "The heathen raged, the kingdoms were moved: he uttered his voice, the earth melted. The Lord of hosts is with us; the God of Jacob is our refuge. . . . Come, behold the works of the Lord, what desolations he hath made in the earth. He maketh wars to cease unto the end of the earth; he breaketh the bow, and cutteth the spear in sunder; he burneth the chariot in the fire. Be still, and know that I am God: I will be exalted among the heathen, I will be exalted in the earth. The Lord of hosts is with us; the God of Jacob is our refuge" (Psalm 46:6-11).

122

CHAPTER 11

THE CAPTAIN OF OUR SALVATION

"And, behold, God himself is with us for our captain" (2 Chronicles 13:12).

"For it became him, for whom are all things, and by whom are all things, in bringing many sons unto glory, to make the captain of their salvation perfect through sufferings" (Hebrews 2:10).

History is filled with the exploits of great military leaders. Joshua, the son of Nun, conqueror of Canaan; Gideon, the Abiezrite, who overwhelmed the Midianites; Nebuchadnezzar, the king-general of Babylon; Cyrus the Persian; Alexander the Great; Pompey of Rome; Napoleon Bonaparte; George Washington; John J. Pershing; Dwight D. Eisenhower; Bernard Law Montgomery; and Norman Schwartzkoff are names that stand out in the history of military conquest and success. A look at their lives and deeds reveals some common threads in their makeup, no matter what period of history they occupied.

First, all great military leaders acquire a thorough knowledge of their enemy. They learn to anticipate his actions and reactions. They know his strengths and weaknesses, and they are constantly aware of the enemy's whereabouts.

Second, these military geniuses are aware of their own strengths and weaknesses, and plan their paths accordingly.

Third, they know when to move forward on the offensive, and they have a keen insight on when to stand their ground and defend their territory.

And finally, they all realize the need of keeping their troops in the best fighting condition possible.

These truths of military leadership remain constant whether the army fights with spears and swords or computer-guided smart bombs.

These characteristics also are true concerning the Captain of our salvation, the Lord Jesus Christ. He is the great leader in spiritual warfare, and beside Him all others are dwarfed.

First, He has a thorough knowledge of the Enemy. Christ was there when Satan and all the angels who fell with him were created. John says, "In the beginning was the Word, and the Word was with God, and the Word was God. The same was in the beginning with God. All things were made by him; and without him was not any thing made that was made" (John 1:1-3). Christ, as a member of the triune Godhead, had a vital role as Creator in the creation of all things, including the anointed cherub Lucifer, who was made perfect in beauty and in wisdom (Ezekiel 28:12-17). God said this anointed cherub was lifted up in pride because of his beauty and had corrupted his wisdom with his brightness. His pride had deceived him (Obadiah 1:3). His desire to ascend above God sealed his doom and destined

THE CAPTAIN OF OUR SALVATION

him for hell (Isaiah 14:12-15). Christ has firsthand knowledge of all this, for He was there when it occurred. Not only that, but He has also been there throughout all eternity. Every day and every hour He is there. He has watched keenly Satan's every move and strategy of conquest. He knows his moods and temperament. He absolutely knows what the Enemy is going to do in any given situation, for Christ is more than the carpenter from Nazareth—He is the living God, and He is omniscient. What a leader we have! He doesn't need intelligence specialists to inform Him of every movement and possible attack that may be developing. He knows! One songwriter wrote, "He knows just what I need!" You can believe that! No military leader who ever lived knows the Enemy better than Christ, for He knows all.

Second, our Captain is aware of His own strengths. He has declared emphatically, "All power is given unto me in heaven and in earth" (Matthew 28:18). No general who ever lived could conquer death and the grave, but Christ did. He did what no man could: He overcame temptation and lived without sin. God has declared He will make all Christ's enemies His footstool (Hebrews 1:13). Christ can lead us confidently in every battle, for He knows His strength.

Third, our Captain knows when to lead us forward and when to stand our guard and defend our place of habitation. Psalm 23 is a beautiful portrait of Christ. Here David portrayed the Lord as a skilled and able shepherd taking care of the sheep in all circumstances. Two verses are especially noteworthy. In verse 4, David said that in the extremely dangerous valleys of our walk with our Shepherd, there is no need to fear evil when our Shepherd is with us. With His staff with the crook in the end, He will guide us lest we wander like

125

sheep who don't watch where they are going. The staff of direction is a comfort. It can turn our heads aright or stop us cold or lift us from the edge of a deadly precipice. How can the rod, an instrument for killing, comfort us? The rod can be used for discipline to punish two stubborn rams who want only to butt heads and fight for dominance, or the rod can crush the skull of the wolf or break the jaw of the jackal who comes to devour the flock. The shepherd has both a staff and a rod, and in the dark, uncertain valleys his strong presence is near even when the enemy lurks in the shadows.

David said in verse 5 that the Shepherd prepares a table for us. Often a shepherd goes ahead of his flock to mountain pastures and carefully looks for poisonous weeds and plants which the sheep might unwittingly eat. He also looks for the tracks of wolves and leopards and the deep imprints left by the paw of a heavy lion or bear. After the pasture is cleared of poisonous plants, the shepherd arms himself with weapons of defense and leads the flock to eat the lush green grass. As they graze contentedly, he puts oil on the heads of injured or ailing sheep. Christ takes care of us!

Finally, He is a great military captain, for He knows how to keep His troops in prime fighting condition. He convicts us of sin lest the disease get a grip on us and weaken our resolve. He encourages us with showers of blessings. He gives us water that causes us never to thirst. And the life he gives is a more abundant life. We go forward, not in the weakness of the flesh but in the power of His might.

Though many great wars have plagued the human race during history, no war ever fought was more important than the war currently being fought in the realm of the spirit.

Our Enemy is old and cunning. He has perfected the

tactics that best bring out his strengths. He is a master of subtlety and deceit. A prayerless soldier with a poor knowledge of the Word and his armor cast aside will fall prey to Satan and his evil forces.

But let us talk no more of the strengths and cunning of our Enemy. It is high time for the church of the living God to take a long and admiring look at our Captain and become so enamored with Him that we beg to be in His service, more than willing to spend our lives in obedience to His every command.

Near the blue waters of the Mediterranean Sea at Caesarea Philippi, Jesus declared not only to His disciples but also to the universe and to the spirit world: "Upon this rock I will build my church; and the gates of hell shall not prevail against it" (Matthew 16:18). The meaning of His declaration, from the original Greek language, is that Jesus is building the church upon Himself—the foundation rock, *petra* (not *petros*, which is a small fragment of rock and the name given to Simon Peter). Christ was saying He would build His church upon the fact He is the Christ, the Son of the living God—and all it means for us subsequently: redemption, regeneration, resurrection, glorification, eternity with God, and the kingdom of God reigning forever.

The reference to "gates of hell" simply means that the power of death itself cannot stop the church Jesus would build. It has not; the church lives on! The church has been persecuted, slaughtered, overtaxed, outlawed, and burned. It has suffered without ceasing, but it remains and grows and flourishes. It shines in deserts and on mountains, in the cold, the damp, and in blistering heat.

When one considers all this, the conclusion quickly is reached that our Leader knows how to conduct a war. We are not a group of wimpy, weak, anemic, beatdown, stomped-on, beleaguered, ready-to-faint conscripts. We have cast off the shackles and burdens of our sin and are ready to march forward. Our armor has been designed by our Captain, and we have put it all on. We have known the agony of fighting in the heat of battle, but with the crown of rejoicing as the goal before us, victory dances in our eyes.

Our captain is Christ Jesus himself, and He has many wonderful attributes that make Him a grand leader of the saints.

He is the *Son of God*. The Greek for *only begotten* means "one of a kind." There is no one else like Jesus. He is unique in all the universe. He has been both God and man. He knows the human experience and can identify with His troops. He once was a wrinkled, wet, newborn baby, and someone tied off His umbilical cord just as they did ours. He was a chubby-fisted, waddling toddler and an excited, tree-climbing, bright-eyed little boy. He was an adolescent, changing from a boy to a man, and He knows the difficulty of life at this juncture. He was a teenager and, then, a young man faced with a mission. He stood on the edge of the wilderness, ready to face 40 days of hunger and an awesome attack from Satan. Our dear Captain has known poverty, hunger, cold, sleeplessness, betrayal, desertion, and false accusations. He has suffered indignities of the worst sort. His rights were denied, and He was the victim of illegal court proceedings. Death, according to the psalmist David, is a valley where shadows abound, and our Captain walked the valley through its fullest extent after leaving a chamber of torture that defies description. The body of our Captain lay on the cold ledge of stone hewn in a tomb while His spirit ministered in paradise. He alone has experienced the glory of glorification, and He lives eternally.

THE CAPTAIN OF OUR SALVATION

According to the Scripture, our Captain was made perfect—completing all heaven's objectives for the Redeemer—through His suffering. He now makes intercession for us (Hebrews 7:25).

He is the perfect Captain to lead us in our spiritual battles, for He knows all about sin. While on earth, He was "in all points tempted like as we are, yet without sin" (Hebrews 4:15). "For even hereunto were ye called: because Christ also suffered for us, leaving us an example, that ye should follow his steps: who did no sin, neither was guile found in his mouth" (1 Peter 2:21, 22).

He is well acquainted with what sin can do, so He has given Himself totally, both then and now, for sin's eradication. *Eradicate* means to "pull up by the roots, utterly destroying." So is Christ's intent toward sin. "For this purpose the Son of God was manifested, that he might destroy the works of the devil" (1 John 3:8).

Does Christ hate sin? According to the Bible, He does: "But unto the Son he saith, Thy throne, O God, is for ever and ever: a sceptre of righteousness is the sceptre of thy kingdom. Thou hast loved righteousness, and hated iniquity" (Hebrews 1:8, 9).

Christ died for sin. Christ's blood is the only thing that can cleanse men from sin. "He that committeth sin is of the devil; for the devil sinneth from the beginning" (1 John 3:8). Christ loves the sinner, but hates the sin. He has the greatest stake in this war of the spirit against the devil. He gave Himself completely, unselfishly, to defeat the devil and the power of sin.

He is the perfect Captain, for He has the attributes of God. He is omnipotent (Matthew 28:18), omniscient (1 John 3:20), and omnipresent (Matthew 28:20). He also is unchangeable (Hebrews 7:24), and He is the epitome of love (Ephesians 3:19).

SPIRIT WARS

Our Captain has a master plan for His followers and for the universe. This plan is foolproof, for it is His declared will. His plan for us as individuals is that we grow in His grace and knowledge (2 Peter 3:18). His plan for the body of Christ corporately is for us to proclaim the biblical truth of God's salvation plan for the entire human family. In short, God wants the message of John 3:16 to get out, for it works (John 12:32).

The Book of Revelation is the revelation of Jesus Christ (1:1). This revelation shows Christ's plan for the end of the church's journey on earth, the judgment of men and nations, and the destruction of the evil satanic system built by the devil. In it, we see the devil's end. As we prepare to look at the final battle, may we be comforted by the glorious truth stated in Romans 8:28: "And we know that all things work together for good to them that love God, to them who are the called according to his purpose."

CHAPTER 12

THE FINAL BATTLE: THE TRIUMPH OF THE LAMB

"Thou hast put all things in subjection under his feet. For in that he put all in subjection under him, he left nothing that is not put under him. But now we see not yet all things put under him" (Hebrews 2:8).

"Then as I looked I heard the voices of countless angels. These were all round the throne and the living creatures and the elders. Myriads upon myriads there were, thousands upon thousands, and they cried aloud: 'Worthy is the Lamb, the Lamb that was slain, to receive all power and wealth, wisdom and might, honour and glory and praise!' Then I heard every created thing in heaven and on earth and under the earth and in the sea, all that is in them, crying: 'Praise and honour, glory and might, to him who sits on the throne and to the Lamb for ever and ever!'" (Revelation 5:11-13, *NEB*).

As biblical prophecy is fulfilled at a swiftly increasing pace, most of the Evangelical world has its mind on

SPIRIT WARS

the reality of the end time. I do not believe that we should become so mesmerized by current events that we try to match all of them with some prophetical writing, nor should we fall into the trap of date setting, based on biblical arithmetic or someone's purported revelation. Scripture warns us to avoid preoccupation with times and seasons. Jesus said, "It is not for you to know the times or the seasons, which the Father hath put in his own power" (Acts 1:7). Christ's intent was to warn them of the dangers of too much attention and time being taken with date setting. Instead, He told them they would receive power when the Holy Spirit came upon them and that they were to be witnesses throughout the world. Christ had already told His disciples, "But of that day and that hour knoweth no man, no, not the angels which are in heaven, neither the Son, but the Father" (Mark 13:32). God's purposes are based on divine and perfect reason. The fact that we don't know when Christ will return and the process of judgment on the earth will begin causes us to guard our hearts and take heed so that we will be ready regardless of the time. This also should give us impetus to work diligently in God's vineyard. We must work "while it is day" (John 9:4).

In this book on spiritual warfare, the reader has become acquainted with many last-day schemes Satan has put into action. Some are obvious to the casual observer. Things strictly forbidden by the Scripture have become so commonplace there is no longer any shock in their observation, but rather a dangerous casual acceptance. The New Age movement, secular humanism, satanism, the occult, the teaching of evolution, the murder of unborn children, the debauchery of satisfying perverted lusts, and the unbridled greed of a materialistic society hardly raise an eyebrow today.

THE FINAL BATTLE: THE TRIUMPH OF THE LAMB

Our society has become akin to the world of Noah and the city of Lot on the eve of their destruction.

Apathy rules in many Evangelical churches, and we have seen a decline of morals and integrity in the clergy. The embarrassment and the shattered lives of ministers who have fallen prey to the devourer has broken the heart of the church of the Lord Jesus. Hell laughs and dances with delight, and some wonder will it ever end.

We need to understand the Bible plainly teaches that the world is not going to get better until Christ comes. Yet some are teaching that Christians will become so numerous and fill the earth with goodness to the point that the kingdom of God will descend. This type of teaching is the last-day heresy Peter and Jude warned about (2 Peter 3:1-10; Jude 4, 16-19).

The Bible teaches, "Evil men and seducers shall wax worse and worse" (2 Timothy 3:13). Christ said the days preceding His return would be like the days of Noah and the days of Lot (Luke 17:26-30). In the days of Noah the earth was corrupt and filled with violence (Genesis 6:11). Men's imaginations were "evil continually" (v. 5). It also was a time of much trade, commerce, and accumulation of wealth. Is the pattern beginning to emerge? It sounds like our modern world, doesn't it?

What about Lot's days? Lot's world also was characterized by much commerce (Luke 17:28). But what stood out about Lot's day was the perversion and homosexuality that ruled the minds of the men of Sodom. They became as savage beasts in their lusts (Genesis 19:4-9). The evil of homosexuality had possessed most of the city, and the tragedy was, it had become accepted. Reading the Genesis account, one has to believe the laws of Sodom did not forbid homo-

133

SPIRIT WARS

sexuality but actually protected the continuance of the perversion. God burned down their city and judged them horribly. No doubt, their cries echo in the chambers of hell this very day.

The Genesis portrait of Sodom and Gomorrah looks like a portrait of our modern world with its tolerance and acceptance of Bible-condemned sin. There are those in Christendom who, like the sons-in-law of Lot, laugh and mock at old-fashioned virtue and the preaching of the forthcoming judgment of God on sin. "Nevertheless the foundation of God standeth sure, having this seal, The Lord knoweth them that are his. And, Let every one that nameth the name of Christ depart from iniquity" (2 Timothy 2:19).

God flooded Noah's world and incinerated Sodom and Gomorrah. God will purge this world with fire and judge it in the caldron known as the Great Tribulation (2 Peter 3:7, 10, 11; Matthew 24:21, 22).

When God has completed His dealing with the earth, and Christ returns to reign for 1,000 years (Zechariah 14:1-9; Revelation 19:11-21; 20:6), two events of note are a twofold stroke of defeat and ultimate damnation for the devil and his forces.

The first is found in Revelation 20. After the battle of Armageddon, a phenomenal event occurs. A mighty angel of God descends (v. 1). In his hand is the key to the bottomless pit and a great chain. He lays hold on the devil, binds him with the chain, casts him into the bottomless pit, and seals the pit. The devil is confined there for 1,000 years, the length of Christ's earthly reign (vv. 2, 3).

Why does this event occur? Why doesn't God just destroy him then and there? We do not want to be so presumptuous as to attempt to decipher the mind of the God of heaven, but I believe there is a great wisdom

134

THE FINAL BATTLE: THE TRIUMPH OF THE LAMB

and truth to be seen in this act of binding and casting the devil into a bottomless pit. The reason may be this: It takes more power to control something than it does to destroy it. God shows the entire universe, and the devil and his followers, He has the power to control the devil. He renders the devil powerless and ineffective for a millennium. The devil's last years of existence are spent falling and tumbling with no foundation to rest upon or to stand.

The second phase of the final battle is found in Revelation 20:7-15. After 1,000 years, the devil is loosed for a short period. He quickly gathers an army made up of Tribulation survivors and their descendants which numbers in the multitudes from many nations. They surround the Holy City, New Jerusalem; and when they do, doom awaits them all. When they lay their siege, a fire comes down from God out of heaven and devours them (v. 9). Verse 10 is the obituary of the devil, the enemy of righteousness: "And the devil that deceived them was cast into the lake of fire and brimstone, where the beast and the false prophet are, and shall be tormented day and night for ever and ever." The balance of chapter 20 deals with the Great White Throne Judgment, at which the wicked dead are judged and cast into the lake of fire.

The apostle Paul said, "God hath chosen the foolish things of the world to confound the wise; and God hath chosen the weak things of the world to confound the things which are mighty" (1 Corinthians 1:27). The one thing that made the defeat of evil possible was the triumph of the Lamb of God. It doesn't make sense, as far as this world is concerned, to mix words like *triumph, victory, conqueror,* and *conquest* with a lamb. But God did this and confounded the mighty powers of hell and all carnal men of the earth who have rejected Christ.

135

SPIRIT WARS

In Christ's time, the Jews of Israel believed firmly in the law of Moses. The institution of the Passover was especially precious to them, for it commemorated so much of what God had done for their nation and for their deliverance.

On the 10th day of the Jewish month of Nisan, which corresponds with our late March or early April, the priests would select a male lamb of the first year that was spotless and without blemish. They would bring it into the courtyard of the Temple, and for the next four days they would inspect it thoroughly. Constantly, descendants of Aaron would be looking carefully over the selected lamb. They would look in his ears, mouth, eyes, and around his hooves. They would examine his wool and feel the contours at the folds of his skin, searching for any blemish that would make the lamb unworthy for sacrifice. On the 14th day of the month of Nisan, at precisely 9 o'clock in the morning, the priest would untie the lamb and take it to the altar of burnt sacrifice. Here the lamb was tied to the horns of the altar according to the commandment of God. The altar was made of acacia wood and overlaid with brass, which was known as the metal of judgment. The lamb lay there until 3 o'clock in the afternoon, a time known as the time between evenings. The Jews had two evening sacrifices, the minor evening sacrifice, or oblation, which was offered between 12 noon and 3 o'clock, and the major oblation, which was offered between 3 o'clock and 6 o'clock. At exactly 3 o'clock the priest would walk up the incline to the top of the altar and kneel with a sharp knife. He would slit the throat of the lamb, killing it almost instantly, and then he would cry with a loud voice, "It is finished!" The lamb was then sacrificed and its blood offered to God in the Holy of Holies for the sins of the people.

THE FINAL BATTLE: THE TRIUMPH OF THE LAMB

On Passover evenings in Jewish homes, the Jewish father would take three loaves of unleavened bread and place them in what was known as a utility bag. From this was drawn the center, or second slice, and it was wrapped in a linen napkin and then hidden in the house. The children then sought for it and when found, they were rewarded with a gift.

Christ, the Lamb of God, entered Jerusalem, the city of His death, before the Passover and was examined during the same time the priests were examining the select lamb. Doctors, lawyers, Pharisees, members of the Sanhedrin, and even the Roman procurator examined Him thoroughly. Pilate, the last examiner, declared, "I find no fault in him" (John 19:6).

While the Jews, at 9 o'clock on the day of the Passover, were tying their lamb to an altar, a man with a mallet was fastening the Lamb of God to a rugged cross. At 3 o'clock that day two lambs died. A cry was heard from a brass altar, "It is finished," and on Golgotha's dark brow the Son of God lifted His voice and cried, "It is finished" (John 19:30). While Jewish fathers throughout Israel hid bread in linen napkins, the Bread of Life, God's Son, was wrapped in linen by Joseph of Arimathea and Nicodemus and buried in a sepulchre hewn in rock. That night, Jewish children searched for unleavened bread in anticipation of a reward when they found it. On the third day, women, disciples, and travelers to Emmaus would be rewarded, for He who had been wrapped in linen would rise to live forevermore!

The Lamb has conquered, and the doom of the devil is sealed for all eternity. Righteousness will triumph. The Word of God, which is established forever, has declared it. The only hope for eternal happiness and real meaning in life is found when Christ is the redeemer of our life and our Lord and Master. Christians who love God and who have given control of their life to Christ will not let the plague and onslaught of satanic attack break them down. May the following scriptures strengthen your resolve, and may you become a Christian whose life is built on the principles of the Word:

"Fear not: for they that be with us are more than they that be with them" (2 Kings 6:16).

"Let God arise, let his enemies be scattered: let them also that hate him flee before him" (Psalm 68:1).

"No weapon that is formed against thee shall prosper; and every tongue that shall rise against thee in judgment thou shalt condemn. This is the heritage of the servants of the Lord, and their righteousness is of me, saith the Lord" (Isaiah 54:17).

"So shall they fear the name of the Lord from the west, and his glory from the rising of the sun. When the enemy shall come in like a flood, the Spirit of the Lord shall lift up a standard against him" (Isaiah 59:19).

"What shall we then say to these things? If God be for us, who can be against us?" (Romans 8:31).

BIBLIOGRAPHY

Anderson, Neil T., and Steve Russo. *The Seduction of Our Children*. Eugene, Ore.: Harvest House Publishers, 1991.

Chandler, Russell. *Understanding the New Age*. Dallas, Texas: Word Publishing, 1991.

Conn, Charles W. *The Anatomy of Evil*. Old Tappan, N.J.: Fleming H. Revell Co., 1981.

French, Joel and Jane. *War Beyond the Stars*. Harrison, Ark.: New Leaf Press, 1979.

Green, Michael. *Exposing the Prince of Darkness*. Ann Arbor, Mich.: Servant Publishers, 1991.

Groothuis, Douglas R. *Unmasking the New Age*. Downers Grove, Ill.: InterVarsity Press, 1986.

Larson, Bob. *New Book of Cults*. Wheaton, Ill.: Tyndale House Publishers, 1989.

Mather, George A., and Larry A. Nichols. *Dictionary of Cults, Sects, Religions and the Occult*. Grand Rapids: Zondervan Publishing House, 1993.

Michaelson, Johanna. *Like Lambs to the Slaughter*: Your Child and the Occult. Eugene, Ore.: Harvest House Publishers, 1989.

Murillo, Mario. *Fresh Fire*. Danville, Calif.: Anthony Douglas Publishing, 1991.

Murphy, Ed. *The Handbook for Spiritual Warfare*. Nashville, Tenn.: Thomas Nelson Publishers, 1992.

Pentecost, J. Dwight. *Your Adversary the Devil*. Grand Rapids: Zondervan Publishing House, 1969.

Stedman, Ray C. *Spiritual Warfare*. Portland, Ore.: Multnomah, 1975.

Taylor, Ian T. *In the Minds of Men*. Toronto: TFE Publishing, 1987.

Tucker, Ruth A. *Another Gospel*. Grand Rapids: Zondervan Publishing House, 1989.

Unger, Merrill F. *Biblical Demonology*. Wheaton, Ill.: Scripture Press Publications, Inc., 1977.

Voorhis, G.D. *Satan Exposed*. Greensboro, N.C.: by G.D. Voorhis, 1973.

Wagner, C. Peter, and F. Douglas Pennoyer. *Wrestling With Dark Angels*. Ventura, Calif.: Regal Books, 1990.

Wagner, C. Peter. *Warfare Prayer*. Ventura, Calif.: Regal Books, 1992.